From
Heartache to
Happiness

– Letting go and moving on –

William W. Stafford
and
Irene T. Stafford

BALBOA.
PRESS

A DIVISION OF HAY HOUSE

Balboa Press books may be ordered through booksellers or by contacting:

Balboa Press
A Division of Hay House
1663 Liberty Drive
Bloomington, IN 47403
www.balboapress.com
1 (877) 407-4847

Because of the dynamic nature of the Internet, any web addresses or
links contained in this book may have changed since publication and
may no longer be valid. The views expressed in this work are solely those
of the author and do not necessarily reflect the views of the publisher,
and the publisher hereby disclaims any responsibility for them.

The author of this book does not dispense medical advice or prescribe the use
of any technique as a form of treatment for physical, emotional, or medical
problems without the advice of a physician, either directly or indirectly. The
intent of the author is only to offer information of a general nature to help
you in your quest for emotional and spiritual well-being. In the event you use
any of the information in this book for yourself, which is your constitutional
right, the author and the publisher assume no responsibility for your actions.

Any people depicted in stock imagery provided by Thinkstock are models,
and such images are being used for illustrative purposes only.
Certain stock imagery © Thinkstock.

Printed in the United States of America.

ISBN: 978-1-4525-9241-1 (sc)
ISBN: 978-1-4525-9242-8 (hc)
ISBN: 978-1-4525-9240-4 (e)

Library of Congress Control Number: 2014902725

Balboa Press rev. date: 3/27/2014

In memory of Shannon who inspired us to walk this path.
And to all of you who are letting go and moving on.

When you learn your lessons, the pain goes away.

—Elisabeth Kübler-Ross

Contents

Acknowledgments xiii

Introduction xv

1: Awareness and Intention 1

Adversity Is Your Ally 1

Loving Is the Purpose 3

Guidelines for Your Journey 4

Intentions 6

Tool 1: How to Set an Intention 7

Inner Reflections 8

2: The Road Ahead 9

The Journey into the Heart 9

The Tornado of Life 12

Cycle of Feelings 14

How It Was for Bill 17

The Neutral Observer 18

Healing Actions 19

Tool 2: Self-Discovery Journal 19

Inner Reflections 20

3: Healing Is a Choice 21

One Step Forward, Two Steps Back 21

What Others Say 25

Triggering Comments 26

How We Felt 27

Avoiding Our Feelings 29

Some Questions Answered 31

Nobody Cares 34
Irene Owning Her Feelings 34
Healing Actions 35
Self-Discovery Journal 35
   Tool 3: Meditation 36
   Cloud Meditation 36
Inner Reflections 37

4: A Lifetime of Loving 38
Choosing To Live 38
Men and Women Process Differently 42
Why Me? 44
Meditation 45
The Life Review Chart 46
The Life Review Instructions 46
   Tool 4: A Lifetime of Loving 48
   Tool 5: Free-Form Writing 49
Healing Actions 51
Self-Discovery Journal 51
Inner Reflections 51

5: Commitment to Self 52
Life Review Awareness 52
Feelings and Patterns 53
Preparing Your Relationship Review 53
Relationship Meditation 55
   Tool 6: Relationship Review 56
Feelings Mapping 57
Reframing Issues as Blessings 59
Reframing Worksheet Instructions 60
   Tool 7: The Reframing Worksheet 61
Narrative from a Past Workshop 62

Healing Actions 63
Self-Discovery Journal 63
The Art of the Reframe 63
Meditation 64

6: I Was Never Enough 65
Unmet Expectations 65
Woulda, Shoulda, Coulda 66
Tool 8: Woulda, Shoulda, Coulda 67
Guilt and Shame 68
Projections and Your Shadow Self 68
Awareness and Compassion Meditation 71
Affirmations 72
Bill's Affirmation 74
Tool 9: Affirmation Worksheet 75
My Affirmations for Living 77
Healing Actions 77
Self-Discovery Journal 77
Woulda, Shoulda, Coulda 78
Affirmations 78
Meditation 78
Meditation 79
Inner Reflections 79

7: Self-Forgiveness 80
Forgiving Others 82
Physical Pain 83
Compassionate Self-Forgiveness 84
Bill's Process 85
The Statements 87
Filling Your Heart with Loving 88
End of the Beginning 89
Tool 10: Self-Forgiveness Worksheet 90

Gratitude 90
Magical Moments 92
Healing Actions 93
    Self-Discovery Journal..........................93
    Meditation..93
Inner Reflections 94

8: Choosing to Be Free and Loving.................96
Letting Go and Moving On.......................96
    Tool 11: Completion Worksheet............98
    Tool 12: A Completion Letter............. 101
    Positive Rituals 102
Commitment to Self.................................103
Healing Actions 103
Inner Reflections 103

9: Conclusion...104
My (New) Life Is Just Beginning 104
    In Conclusion 104
    Next Steps..105

10: Our Journey...107

Acknowledgments

We are grateful to all of the individuals who, over the last decade, have trusted us to guide them through their life transitions in our workshops and private coaching practice. Their courage to go deep and heal from within inspires us to continue on this path.

A deep and heartfelt thanks to John C. Stafford for his calm and masterful editing of this book and his wise feedback.

Our gratitude to Thomas for his love and patience with us over the years as we navigated through our own learnings and discovered the true meaning of unconditional love.

Thank you, Irene, for holding a place of integrity through the process of this book and for the journey of love we have traveled together. I am eternally grateful for your love and companionship.

Thank you, Bill, for your unconditional love and support through the darkness and into the light. My heart is filled with gratitude for the magical life we have created together and for your courage and commitment to lead the way.

To all of our family members, friends, and acquaintances, thank you for choosing to be part of our lives. Without the experiences we have shared together, this book would not have been possible.

Introduction

L et's be honest—heartache sucks! It doesn't feel good and we don't like it. But the reality is, it's a part of life. What if every issue in our lives that we view as negative was actually a wake-up call, a way to get our attention? When you open up your heart and let yourself feel all your feelings, you not only feel the pain but give yourself permission to have more joy and love in your life.

What we have outlined in this book is just the beginning of your journey into healing your heart. It is a journey that we have made. This is not simply a set of exercises that you do once and put away. It is a new way of relating to yourself as you navigate through all of the issues of life. It's a practical philosophy for living a more peaceful, successful, and loving life.

We offer a few suggestions. It is not enough just to read this book. It is not a narrative. It's a set of carefully designed tools and skills to assist you in moving from heartache to happiness. So do each of the exercises as fully and completely as possible, but don't get stuck on any one exercise. You can always go back and fill in more detail later.

We highly recommend that you take a minimum of six weeks to work through all of the material in this book. You are learning lifelong skills. After you have completed the exercises, go back and begin again. You will have a higher perspective and an opportunity to deepen your practice after you've worked through the exercises once.

Finally, do not judge yourself too harshly, preferably not at all. What we have learned from our research and working with clients over the last decade is that most people have never been taught successful tools and skills for processing and releasing all of the inevitable ups, downs, and turmoil that come with life. Be gentle with yourself. Reach out to others. You never need to go it alone.

The right time to do this work is now. You don't have to wait to feel better emotionally or physically. In our experience, what stops people from moving forward is fear. There is no better time than the present. Give yourself permission to begin now. When you've completed the work in this book, you'll be glad you took the time to value your own healing.

1

Awareness and Intention

The best and most beautiful things in the world cannot be seen
or even touched. They must be felt with the heart.

—Helen Keller

Adversity Is Your Ally

We didn't like the way we were feeling. We had become
aware of the numbness in our lives. The feeling, or lack
of feeling, was all pervasive. Just one foot in front of the other,
looking down, not seeing ahead, focusing only on the next step,
the next thing to do. We were living on automatic pilot. This was
just a shell of existence: pretending to be alive.

We had been to a lot of support groups and found many programs that didn't work for us. So we set upon a journey to find a way to heal our heartache, to find the tools that would assist us in moving through all of our experiences with loss and other issues. What we found was light years beyond what we had ever imagined. We found a life filled with more joy, wonder, and loving than we could have dreamed. Not only did we heal our most present heartache, we discovered other issues we had been totally unaware of. They were holding us back in our relationships with ourselves and others.

In our search, both internally and in the physical world, we found what worked for us and began to share our work with others. Every experience of loss and heartache is unique, as is each person's responses and reactions. We have outlined the tools and techniques that worked for us as we navigated our personal heartaches. These are the same tools and techniques we use today with our coaching clients. They are effective if you do the work from the inside out.

We are not telling you what is true, only what we have found helpful. We encourage you to commit fully to experiencing the exercises in this book. Use what works for you and let go of the rest. Set aside those things that don't seem to be a "fit" for you at this time and try them on later. What doesn't work for you today may make more sense at another time or when you look at it from a different perspective.

Throughout this book we invite you to examine your life and your experiences with those you love, those you may now consider as less than loved ones, and most importantly, with yourself. In particular, we will help you identify those people and events that hold the most meaning for you, have the deepest feelings, and with whom you continue to invest energy, both loving and painful.

We will show you how to find the lessons, opportunities, and blessings in these experiences, identifying and releasing you from the judgments you might have made and coming to a place of gratitude for the learning and loving that these people have made in your life.

Loving Is the Purpose

We have learned that the healing of all issues must be cleared on the four levels of existence: physical, mental, emotional, and spiritual. Achieving balance on all four of these levels is essential. They are not separate entities, but interrelated parts of the whole person.

The experiences you see as negative are not mistakes or punishments; they are actually an integral part of the life journey. Our issues are not healed at the same level as they were created. Healing occurs only when we are able to view them from a higher and more loving perspective. We use the words Spirit, God, or Christ Consciousness interchangeably. In this book we use the phrase *spiritual source*. The specific words are not as important as you finding the meaning in them. If you are uncomfortable with the words we use, please feel free to substitute words that work for you.

The spiritual wound can be the most difficult to work with. Many people we have worked with have felt great anger at Spirit for the loss they have suffered. Anger exacerbates the feelings of separation and abandonment in our lives. We may feel we are alone, that we have to do it all ourselves, and yet our feelings of abandonment may not allow us to move forward.

These feelings feed upon themselves and become our core issues. It is probably not productive to work with these fundamental issues directly in the beginning. The good news is that as you use our process to work on all of your other issues, these feelings will begin to loosen.

Take heart and be gentle with yourself. If a child skinned her knee, you wouldn't poke the wound with your finger, would you? You would kiss it and apply a generous amount of loving. We suggest you do the same with yourself.

This book is about moving into loving as opposed to sustaining the feelings of heartache and loss. We will fully support you processing through your present heartache as a necessary part of the journey to a life filled with more joy, peace, connection, and loving.

Guidelines for Your Journey

> You do not know the road ahead of you: You are committing your life to a way.
>
> —Ralph Waldo Emerson

We only have four basic guidelines. These are principles we try to live in our own lives. We are works in progress. When we forget, we try to let that go and get back on track.

If the only thing you learn from this book is to integrate these principles into your way of being, your life will automatically be filled with more happiness and loving and less suffering and judgment. These principles create a foundation for living. We call them *guidelines* as opposed to *rules*. Broken rules tend to create negative judgments. Our guidelines are a firm direction. When we "break" a guideline, we simply take corrective actions to get back on track.

1. Commitment to Self

We often treat others with more care and compassion than we are willing to give ourselves. Be at least as kind, gentle, and respectful to yourself as you are to others. Schedule time every day for each of these areas (they are all connected):

Physical exercise
Mental stimulation
Emotional cleansing
Spiritual connection

2. Do more of what works and less of what doesn't.

Often, through habit or lack of awareness, we continue patterns or behaviors that do not serve our highest good. In the long run it takes less effort to change them than to continue with self-defeating behaviors.

3. Use everything for your growth and learning.

Every experience in life, whether we hold it as good or bad, joyous or tragic, contains the opportunity to grow in awareness, wisdom, and compassion. It is not the event itself but what we do with it.

4. Practice the art of inner peace.

In order to have more happiness, joy, and peace in our lives, we must first have this intention and practice the art of inner peace every day. The tools for this art include: purpose, equanimity, acceptance, compassion, and engagement.

Intentions

Setting your intention is an important way for you to focus your attention and energy. It is not a commitment to any specific action. You can choose to alter course at any time you feel appropriate. A clear, positive intention comes directly from your true heartfelt purpose and desires.

Think of an intention as a road map. We choose a destination and begin the journey to reach that destination. There are often many ways to get to where we are going, with interesting side trips available. At times we can become so enamored with the side trips, we may never reach our intended destination. Intentions are subconscious reminders of the original purpose of the journey.

Setting an intention is an important process under any circumstances, but it is particularly important when you are moving into deep inner-healing work. It is easy to get distracted, and when we are working with difficult situations or emotions, we will often meet resistance within ourselves. Sometimes we would rather do anything than the emotional cleansing we know needs to be done.

So in a journey through inner healing, we will often encounter fear and resistance. Fear may trigger an inner roadblock and send us onto a side road, away from our original goal: healing an inner wound or conflict. A clear, positive intention is a gentle reminder of what we originally intended to do. There are no negative judgments in an intention.

How often do we make our lives harder than they need to be and put obstacles in our way? Sometimes we are our own worst enemy. The work ahead need not be as hard as we may have thought it would be. We recommend that as part of any intention, you add that it be done with grace and ease.

Not only is intention your purpose and drive to create, it tunes into the power of your spiritual source. There is a place beyond our minds, beyond our egos or personas, that can assist us in achieving our heartfelt dreams and aligning with what is truly in our highest good. Trust or faith is all that is required. Let go of the thought that you need to know how to do it. Trust that when the time is right, the path will become clear and you will be open to seeing and have the courage to act.

Tool 1: How to Set an Intention

Close your eyes and place your hands over your heart. Take in and release several full breaths and center yourself in your heart. Release any judgments about not knowing how to do this or about doing it "right."

The more you practice, the clearer it will become. As with many of the practices in this book, you can't know how from your mind or brain; it comes from "that still small voice inside." What is the outcome you are looking for at this time? Keep breathing and say sentences out loud until you are comfortable with your clear, positive intention.

Setting your intention is an important way for you to choose the direction you want to go with healing your heartache. It is not a commitment to any specific action. You can choose to alter your course at any time.

Your intention can also be done as a writing practice.

Example 1: My intention is to discover issues and upsets that I am holding onto and to release them, so that I can be free and move forward in my life with more peace, joy, happiness, and loving.

Example 2: My intention for this week is to remain centered, being aware of any and all judgments that I place on myself and others.

What is your intention for your growth and healing this week?

Inner Reflections

If you could be free of your past hurts, upsets, or programming, how would your life be different? What would change? How would you be or feel different? What would you have to let go of?

2

The Road Ahead

This we know: All things are connected like the blood which unites one family. All things are connected. Whatever befalls the earth befalls the sons of the earth. Man did not weave the web of life. He is merely a strand of it. Whatever he does to the web he does to himself.

—Chief Seattle

The Journey into the Heart

Everything is connected to everything else. Every thought, feeling, sensation, and experience is connected. Your feelings today are connected to every experience you have ever had. Heartache is a natural response to loss. You are not broken. You don't need to be fixed. Heartache, loss, and change are a normal, natural part of living. Time does not heal all wounds. When we work with the appropriate tools and take care to deal with one issue at a time, healing is not only possible, but a natural response.

One of the deepest purposes of the human experience is to actually feel our feelings and to heal our wounds. Unfortunately, in our society most of us were never taught how to resolve the emotional wounds from heartache and loss. These feelings are often covered up. We don't talk about them in public. We don't talk about them in private.

It is a misconception that the only time we need to work through difficult or uncomfortable feelings is when we are grieving the death of a loved one. Anytime you experience an upset or loss of any kind, you have the opportunity to resolve your inner conflicts and release baggage you have been carrying around, often unconsciously. The loss of confidence, loss of freedom, loss of a job, or even seemingly positive events such as a graduation or retirement can bring up issues of loss. Feelings of heartache or loss can result from an unlimited number of various experiences that happen to us. Even for those who have suffered the same type of loss, each individual experience of that loss is unique.

When an event in your life triggers feelings of heartache or loss, remember that it isn't an isolated event. It is connected to every other experience in your life. That is one of the reasons why everyone's experience with heartache is unique. It is filtered through all of our other life experiences. If the current event touches one of our core issues, it can be debilitating. Core issues of abandonment, unworthiness, betrayal, and victim consciousness are common, perhaps even universal.

It is impossible to separate our lives into neat little boxes. Life comes at us from all sides; and every event, every thought, every emotion is connected to everything else. It can feel overwhelming.

All of us have issues we deal with every day. Much of the time they occur under the surface, and we are unaware of them or how they are affecting our lives. Often they are the same issues or themes, day after day. If we don't resolve an issue when it first arises, life has a way of bringing that issue back to us time and time again until it gets our attention.

One of the central purposes of life is to heal our issues. Remember, an issue is anything that disturbs our peace. If we don't get it the first time, we will always get another opportunity. Often the issues become increasingly intense just to make sure they get our attention. Unresolved issues are a major contributor to holding us back from experiencing a happier and more loving life.

Subconsciously, we are programmed to heal our issues. Something inside us—our souls, if you like—wants to heal, wants to be free and loving. We begin our lives as loving beings, and it is our purpose to rediscover that loving place that exists inside. Our challenge is to rediscover that voice and reconnect with its wisdom. This is the voice of loving: our authentic self. It is the authentic you yearning to be free, to be heard and brought into the light and given power and voice.

When we are able to reconnect with that place inside, there is no fear or confusion. There is no anger, resentment, or judgments. All of our false personas fall away. This is the place of our loving souls. Wisdom, courage, equanimity reside here, along with love and forgiveness.

In this book we will share with you the opportunity for deep healing work. True healing occurs only when we work through our issues on the physical, mental, emotional, and spiritual levels. The exercises in this book have mental aspects, but for true healing you must venture courageously through all of the realms.

The Tornado of Life

You may sometimes feel that you are trapped inside a tornado, flung around and pushed down into the darkness. There is hope, a lifeline, if you will. You do not need anyone else to lift you out of the darkness and into the light of day. Everything you need is already inside you. You just need to learn how to access your inner resources for healing. The only heart you can heal is your own. How you live your life is a choice. As one of our mentors, Dr. Ron Hulnick of the University of Santa Monica, says, "Healing is the application of loving to the parts inside that hurt."

You don't need to learn loving. It is our natural state of being. Our challenge is to learn how to release those things that get in the way, the issues that cover up our abilities to give and receive love.

This may be your opportunity to begin to peel back those layers of the onion, the layers comprised of years of loss and heartache. It may seem hard and scary, but you do it only one layer, one issue, at a time. With each layer you release, your life becomes a little lighter and that much more worth living.

Reading this book is not the same thing as doing the work. You can read all the books you want until the end of time and you may never heal a single issue. Reading and talking are mental exercises. Our pain and suffering exist on the emotional level, in addition to the mental. Our mental and emotional selves often have different agendas. Learning is a mental exercise while healing is an emotional and spiritual experience. Our spiritual selves want to heal, but our minds don't want to go there. We can be amazingly creative on the mental realm to avoid our emotional work. Eating, reading, watching TV, shopping, abusing drugs and alcohol are all ways in which we avoid our pain.

In order to live a healthy, happy, joyful, and loving life we must resolve and heal our issues. The techniques are simple. There is no way to work with all of our issues at one time. That would be overwhelming and impossible. We can only work with one issue at a time, one small step at a time.

How we were raised, the experiences we had growing up and as adults, the heartaches and losses we have suffered all factor in to how we experience and handle loss in the present. Remember, everything is connected to everything else. Every one of our thoughts, emotions, issues, and judgments are connected in some way, though usually under the surface. We are very dynamic beings.

One of the difficulties is that as humans, we like to have routines. We feel safe in continuity. We seek to know what is coming next. The reality we don't want to deal with is that change is constant. That may seem like a paradox, change being constant. We want to hold onto the illusion that we are in control in our lives, but in reality everything is moving, always changing. When we add heartache to our lives, it can feel overwhelming. This can be a natural response to any kind of loss. It is the definition of heartache—the feelings overwhelm us. There is too much input at one time.

We hold onto patterns even when they no longer serve our highest purpose, or even when they are self-destructive.

Cycle of Feelings

The diagram on page 16 is a visual representation of how we process feelings. Human beings are too dynamic to live in assigned, designated boxes. You may have experienced shock, numbness, or the sensation of being overwhelmed. Feelings and judgments don't often flow consistently around the circle. We often bounce back and forth from one feeling to another, from one moment to the next. Often people don't experience denial at all. We know what happened to us. We are not denying it; we just wish it would go away. Denial comes in the form of denying our feelings.

In an ideal world, exploration and integration would follow and bring us back into our normal lives. Wouldn't it be wonderful if life worked that way? In reality, heartache is much more complicated than that. You can be in shock one minute, angry the next, happy a minute after that, and then right back into shock. One day you feel all right and the next you want to pull the covers up over your head and not get out of bed.

This can go on for years. If you don't take the action steps necessary to release your pain and suffering, it can go on for the rest of your life. There are definite action steps you can take that will assist you in moving through your heartache. Bit by bit, layer by layer, issue by issue, you can release pain, suffering, judgment, resentment, and all the other myriad feelings and emotions that keep your loving locked away. It only requires the right tools, courage, and commitment: commitment to yourself, commitment to healing.

Some people believe that if their loss is the loss of a child, they will never heal and be whole again. This is not necessarily so. Let me say this again—you can heal and lead a loving and joyful life no matter what your loss, even if it is that of a child. People may say they won't heal out of fear, guilt, shame, or ignorance. Their fear may be so great they can't ever imagine living through this loss, so they just shut down and bury their feelings. Do not judge the significance of your or someone else's loss as more or less painful. Everyone experiences their pain at 100 percent.

Many people have lived so much of their lives carrying the pain and scars from their childhoods, they might have never had the authentic experience of a love-filled life. Their wounds are so deep, there is no room for them to love themselves.

After the death of a loved one, separation or divorce, or other major loss, your heart is tender and open. It's a great opportunity for you to heal your patterns and feelings associated with this loss and those losses you have experienced throughout your entire life.

Cycle of Feelings

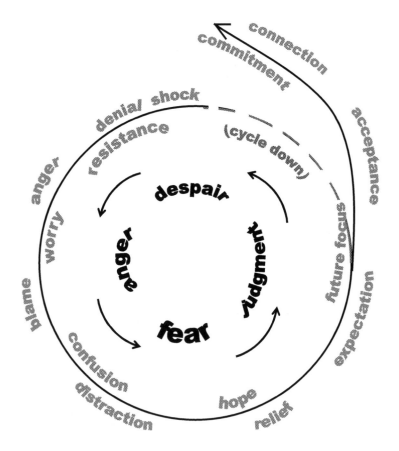

How It Was for Bill

After the death of our daughter, many people, even some well-meaning health-care professionals, looked at us like we were broken forever, never to experience joy again. I believe, without a doubt, that this was only a reflection of their inner fears and limiting beliefs.

I wasn't aware I carried the heartache of the death of my father into my adult life. It was just part of who I thought I was: a somewhat damaged, unlovable individual. I lived with this extra weight, carrying it as part of my personal identity. I was sensitive and deeply loving, but I hid that from others and myself. The positive benefit was when Shannon became ill, I was able to bring some compassion and understanding to the experience.

When she died we moved forward the best we could. Over the years others would say how well we were doing, what a great marriage we had. But underneath, unwilling to admit it even to myself, I was angry, bitter, and resentful. I felt alone. In reality, in addition to the loss of Shannon, old feelings and patterns from past heartaches that I had yet to resolve were resurfacing.

As I later learned, unresolved issues and patterns are often buried deep within us. They don't go away on their own. With each new upset in my life, these feelings grew stronger and louder. As I stated earlier, we are programmed in the direction of healing. Unresolved issues want to surface and be healed. Subconsciously, we don't want to carry these burdens the rest of our lives. Until we acknowledge and begin the healing process, we live with this inner conflict; healing, or holding onto pain and suffering. Sometimes we engage in self-destructive behaviors to numb our inner voices and feelings.

It wasn't until Irene and I separated that I got it. That was finally my wake-up call. I got it: it wasn't about Irene at all. I hated the way I felt and needed to find a way to heal myself, from the inside. I needed to find a way to accept and love myself. Instead of looking for others to validate me and make me feel worthy, I began the inner journey to find ways to bring more loving to myself.

The Neutral Observer

Whatever comes up in your thoughts or emotions, simply take note of it. There is no need to judge it as right or wrong, good or bad. Practicing the art of the neutral observer allows us to step outside of our stories. The journal is a tool we use to practice the art of non-judgment.

The self-discovery journal is a reminder to be the reporter of your life. What did this person you call *me* see, hear, touch, taste, and feel? Report on your own life as if you were standing outside of yourself, watching from a higher perspective.

For example, you might report that in a group setting where you didn't know anyone, you either engaged or held back. If others were expressing opinions you did not agree with, did you speak up or sit silently? What tends to push your buttons? What are your triggers?

If I say, "I saw you flirting with a man at the party last night," that is not an observation. It is a judgment. "I saw you talking to a man at the party last night" is the observation. If I add, "I felt like you were flirting with him," I am expressing my feeling. I am owning it. There is no accusation. Notice, too, that there is no judgment. I stated what I saw and expressed how I felt. When

I communicate to someone what I saw and how I felt, the other person is less likely to become defensive.

What we are doing here is looking for patterns. Where am I in judgment? In this example, it has nothing to do with the other person. It is all within me. The thought or assumption that she was flirting may reveal my feelings of insecurity or unworthiness in relationships, or in general. Perhaps it reveals something in my past that says I don't trust myself, so I am going to project it onto her. Instead of accusing her of something, I am reporting on myself. When you do *X,* I feel *Y.*

We are trying to connect the mental and emotional parts of us. Most of the time they live in two separate realities and are in conflict with each other. Part of our journey is to bring all of the levels of existence—mental, emotional, physical, and spiritual—into harmony with one another.

Healing Actions

Tool 2: Self-Discovery Journal

Begin writing in your self-discovery journal. Remember to become present with yourself. Don't filter or censor your thoughts or feelings, just let them flow directly from your heart, through your hand, and onto the page.

If you do not have our self-discovery journal, purchase some sort of bound journal. Even a spiral notebook will do nicely. Part of the purpose of this journal is to detach from your judgments of right or wrong, good or bad, and begin to learn the practice of viewing life as a neutral observer.

We recommend that you do this exercise at the end of the day. Don't spend more than ten to twenty minutes. You might start by writing about what you experienced with your five senses: what you saw, what you heard, what you tasted, what you smelled, or what you felt with your hands or body.

Next, spend a few minutes writing about your thoughts of the day. Did you notice any patterns to these thoughts?

Finally, write about your emotions and feelings. Try to detach from judging your emotions. You might try thinking of yourself as an ace reporter: just the facts as you see them. Or close your eyes and picture yourself in a movie theater. Review your emotions of the day as if you were watching a movie about some other character.

Inner Reflections

What would it mean to you if you were able to detach from the emotions of a situation and view it as if through the eyes of a reporter?

Have you become aware of any patterns that you are holding onto that no longer serve your highest good?

What would it mean to you if you were able to experience more loving in your life?

Are you able to give more of this to yourself?

What is your intention for your life direction?

3

Healing Is a Choice

No one can make you feel inferior without your consent.
—Eleanor Roosevelt

One Step Forward, Two Steps Back

Most people live in only a small range of their potential. We get used to the way our lives are. It feels like home, no matter how dysfunctional it may be. We become comfortable in our discomfort. We would rather stay in our comfort zone than risk moving forward and growing. It often takes a traumatic event in our lives, like loss and heartache, to get our attention and present us with the opportunity to grow. Often people accept a slow, downward spiral, not really aware that they are piling more and more issues onto their shoulders.

Sometimes it takes a dramatic wake-up call to get our attention. Everyone has a choice to continue moving down toward sadness and pain, or up toward a life of happiness and loving. We just need the right tools and the courage to use them. Not choosing is also a choice. It allows others to choose for us, perpetuating victim consciousness.

Look at the choice diagram on page 24. Where do you see yourself in this energy field? Are you moving up or down? You have the power to choose to move up in the energy continuum to a more loving life. It is a step-by-step process. Simple steps forward, continued over time, reap huge rewards.

We are either expanding, moving to higher levels of consciousness and loving in our lives, or we are contracting, experiencing life at less than full measure. It is as simple as breathing in and breathing out. Is life a joy to be lived or a burden to be endured? The choice is up to each of us alone. No one can make us feel loved, and no one can make us feel unlovable without our permission.

When you move in the direction of loving, you will tend to experience more optimism, lightness, hope, and feelings of possibility. This is regardless of where you are on the continuum of feelings. Even if you are going through a devastating heartache, if you are able to turn your present awareness in a more positive direction, you will experience at least some relief. The future holds possibilities. Whatever you are experiencing presently, if you are able to view it from a positive perspective, you will rise to a higher and more loving experience.

Conversely, even if you are experiencing peace, if you turn your awareness toward a negative point of view, your experience of life will become degraded. Life is a continuous series of transitions. There may be losses and setbacks; there may be major successes. All of those transitions take us out of our comfort zone and cause a certain amount of upset. It isn't the event that is important; it is how we handle and resolve these transitions that is important. Every event in our lives holds the seed of opportunity for healing and growth.

Choice

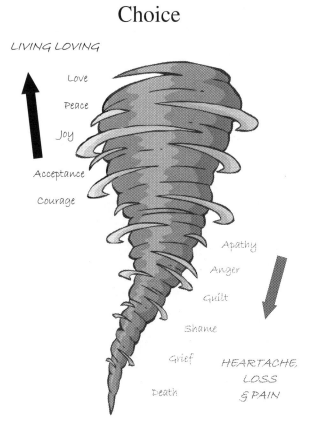

LIVING LOVING

Love

Peace

Joy

Acceptance

Courage

Apathy

Anger

Guilt

Shame

Grief

Death

HEARTACHE,
LOSS
& PAIN

What Others Say

What do you say when there really is nothing to be said? Our friends and family are doing the best they can, but their words can still sting. When we are under stress and our hearts are tender and open, others' comments often trigger our emotions. We are unable, at that time, to hear what they are saying from their perspective.

Often what people are trying to communicate to us is that they don't want to see us suffer. Our suffering makes them uncomfortable or it triggers unresolved grief, guilt, or shame in them. What they are saying underneath their words may be, "I love you, but I don't really know what to say or do."

Sometimes the most loving thing someone can do for us at these times is just to *be* with us and say nothing. A loving hug can be more powerful than any words.

"I know exactly how you feel." When someone would say that to me, I could feel my muscles tense. I would often hold my breath and I would think—or sometimes say—"No, you don't know exactly how I feel. How could you? You're not me. You don't walk in my shoes. You don't know my history or my relationship with that person." Perhaps it would have been more helpful if the other person had said, "I can only imagine what you are going through and I can share what it was like for me, based upon my own experiences."

Triggering Comments

What others say often does have an effect on how we live and feel about ourselves. Others' words can activate unresolved issues from deep inside, or plant the seeds of new issues and heartache. In order to be truly free, we need to bring our conscious attention to the messages we receive from all sources, so that we can process them in a clean and healthy way. By becoming aware of how the incoming message makes us feel, we begin to reclaim our inner power and take true dominion over our lives.

Make a list of some of the comments that people have made that have upset you. Some examples might include:

On Divorce

- You can do better.
- You're making a mistake.
- It's about time.
- The children will suffer.
- He/She's a …
- You should never have married him/her.
- Move on and get over it.
- There are plenty of fish in the sea.

On Death

- You're still young – you can have another child.
- They're in a better place.
- Don't cry – you'll make me sad.
- At least you have another child.
- Stay busy and don't think about it.
- They wouldn't want you to be sad.
- It's been long enough.
- It was meant to be.
- Stay strong.
- You can always get a new one.

How We Felt

A dear friend was distressed because I had asked my husband for a separation. Instead of a friend's support, I was confronted with judgment. My friend said to me, "You'll never find another man who loves you as much as he does." She had decided what was right and wrong, and was trying to convince me I was making a mistake. In her view, Bill and I getting back together would magically resolve all of our problems.

I told her, "But I don't want to get back together with him." And the conversation ended. I left feeling like I had disappointed her, like I was the bad guy, the one who was causing all the problems. It was as if other people were so concerned about their own feelings, whatever had surfaced for them in light of my separation, they really didn't care about what I was going through. It was about making them feel better.

For the first time in my life (or at least it seemed that way), I was standing up for myself. I was doing what I believed was best for me. Sure, it was a risk, but if I didn't take the risk, I believed things would be the same for the rest of my life.

* * *

When a close relative called after she heard that my daughter had cancer, I decided to take the call on the outdoor phone away from the children. I immediately began crying as I told her what the doctor had said. The first thing she told me was, "Don't cry, you'll make me cry." I had to hold my feelings inside to make her feel okay. It didn't matter what my feelings were, she didn't want to hear about them.

* * *

I was walking into the church for the funeral of one of my best friends. As soon as I saw her sister, I began to cry. I was told to stop crying. They would have none of that today.

I held my feelings inside to make other people feel okay. I couldn't believe that I was instructed at a funeral not to cry. When I looked over at the family, they all seemed to be smiling. It was as if they had worn masks so everyone would think they were okay. Was I the only who was sad? For me, sadness and emotions are not signs of weakness. I have learned not to judge my feelings, but rather to allow myself to feel my feelings and not stuff them away.

*   *   *

After my father died, a well-meaning uncle pulled me aside and said, "You're the man of the house now. You have to take care of your mother." Just a couple of hours earlier I had been falling down, trying to learn how to roller skate, and now I was the man of the house. Where did my childhood go?

I've had difficulty sleeping for as long as I can remember. Sometimes it took me two or three hours to fall asleep at night, to finally give in to fatigue. I tossed and turned most of the night, pushing the covers off the bed. As a result, I was late nearly every day of high school. This was a real problem for me. I judged myself harshly for it.

A few years ago, while I was doing an intensive self-examination, I remembered another thing my uncle had said to me. In an effort to be comforting, he said, "Your dad didn't suffer. It was as if he had just gone to sleep." It finally clicked. I wanted to be like my dad, so no wonder I had trouble sleeping. In my mind, if I went to sleep, I would die. Going to sleep equaled death. No wonder I couldn't fall asleep!

When people say things that upset us, that's information that we have something inside that needs to be healed or resolved. They have given us the opportunity to look inside, come into alignment, and release negative energy that we might have been holding onto for a long time. It is not the comments of others that we need to focus on, but the feelings we carry. What feelings are you holding onto and where did they come from?

Avoiding Our Feelings

One of the most common ways we deal with our feelings is to avoid them. It would seem natural to avoid anything that is unpleasant. Unfortunately, many of our upsets and hurt feelings don't go away on their own. We just bury them, on top of all of our other unresolved conflicts. Buried feelings don't die; they fester.

Avoidance behaviors are temporary bandages. Sometimes it's necessary to protect a wound until we are strong enough to heal it. After a while, though, we don't notice how we are avoiding our troubles, and the avoidance becomes an unconscious pattern. Before we can dig into our issues, we need to discover how we are habitually avoiding them. We need to interrupt this pattern so that we can work directly on the issues and resolve them.

Many of our behaviors are benign, but some are downright unhealthy. We would be better served to find new tools to get to the root of our issues and deal with them permanently. The purpose of this work is to teach you new tools, and ways of being with yourself, in order to settle the past and to handle each new upset that comes up in your life, before they have a chance to take root.

Below are some examples of ways we avoid our feelings:

- Eating
- Anger
- Fantasy (movies, TV, books)
- Judgment of others/self
- Serial relationships
- Using alcohol/drugs
- Exercise
- Isolation
- Busyness
- Shopping

These behaviors are unconscious ways we avoid dealing with our most uncomfortable feelings. They are how we protect ourselves from pain. These behaviors may have served a purpose in the past, but now you can learn much more effective ways to process your feelings.

Make a list of all of the things you do to hide from or avoid your feelings. You may want to come back to this list later and add other behaviors as you uncover them.

For each of the avoidance behaviors on your list, add something that you think would be healthier. You are not committing to any changes; you are just exploring other options.

Example: When I feel like eating a quart of ice cream, I could do two minutes of deep breathing.

As you make your list, what feelings come forward? Can you remember other times in your life when you felt this way? Do you notice any patterns?

Some Questions Answered

What follows is a sampling of the questions that often arise in our workshops. It is a composite of different conversation we have had with various participants over the years.

JIM: After my father died, my mother said that I was her reason for living. I was so pissed at her, because I knew what that meant. That I had to somehow be something for her. And she just checked out after that. She couldn't deal with it. I was sort of set up, being told that I had to take care of my mother. But my mother couldn't receive, so one of the patterns I see is being with women where I feel like I should be responsible for their happiness and they can't receive it.

Observing myself from a point of neutrality has been very hard. I'm like a yo-yo right now. One moment I just want to be over it, move on, and be okay, and the next moment I'm so angry at my wife and at what happened. I want to let her know about it and forget about all that spiritual stuff. I want to write her and make sure she is miserable forever.

BILL: It sounds like you are trying to resist these seemingly conflicting thoughts and feelings. What if it were okay to be with this conflict for a while, even embrace the upset? You seem to be unconsciously trying to bring completion to your past relationship. You are on the right track. We call this "completing unfinished business." Practically, internally, and energetically, we do not recommend that you call her.

JIM: I actually did write a letter to my wife about all this stuff. I showed it to a friend. My friend said it sounded kind of angry. It felt kind of good, though. Very therapeutic. I haven't sent it.

BILL: Exactly. You were purging yourself of a lot of negative energy. Don't go back and reread it. Burn it. Literally burn it. You don't want that energy back in you.

[This is the process of free-form writing. It is moving the emotional energy out of your inner self. You want all of those feelings to go out and onto the page. If you reread what you write, you take them right back in. Burn that page up along with those toxic, hateful feelings. If you burn them up, they can't come back in. Who are those feelings hurting anyway? Not the person they are directed at; that person is not here in front of you. They are turned back upon ourselves.]

JIM: It's just so hard because I have my times when I can see the opportunity in this and I feel that I am going to have a good future.

BILL: You are moving through a lifelong pattern activated by your recent loss. Be gentle with yourself. You are doing the best that you can in this present moment. Embrace the conflict. You can even say to yourself, "I see hope for the future, and I'm really pissed off."

JIM: There are other times when that just feels like pie in the sky. You know, like I'm in the depths of something horrible, and I have no faith that there is something better coming.

IRENE: It's two steps forward and one step back. It's not a straight line. And how can you not feel something? You had a relationship with your wife; you shared many years of your life together. How can you move forward and not feel anything?

BILL: If you did, you would be lying to yourself. Some people do this. They say, "Oh, no, I'm fine. Everything's fine," often through clenched teeth, or followed by a heart attack or some other physical ailment. Anyone ever been a smoker? After years of smoking you quit, and you suffer through withdrawal symptoms. Regardless of the type of relationship you had, you are bound to have withdrawals at the end, physically, emotionally, and spiritually. You become used to turning and the other person is there, whether you want them there or not. It has become a conditioned response. Now who do you talk to or argue with?

JIM: That's exactly what I'm going through. There are times when I'll be at work and I get intensely involved with these projects. This is all still pretty new. I'll be working and I'll kind of go into that zone, first with the project and then I'll kind of zone out for a minute. Somehow, in my mind I am thinking, just for an instant, that I'm going to go home and she is going to be there. We'll hug each other. We'll make dinner together, you know the way it was for so long. And then I realize, *no*. Oh, wait a minute, and then the pain becomes intense.

BILL: Everything is energy. Thoughts are like little packets of energy. They are stored in your unconsciousness. They might have been trying to tell you something, not about her necessarily, but something about yourself. When you are going through any growing or healing process or a heartache, you can take the emotional charge off it, but you never forget. You were married for eleven years; you have a lot of energy invested in that relationship. Those are memories that you will have forever. But what is the importance you place on them? It's the emotional charge that you have given to them that we are working with here.

William W. Stafford

Nobody Cares

In the past, Irene held the belief that nobody cared.

Throughout most of my life, I didn't know I wasn't feeling my feelings. I thought I was a normal person. When I was a child, I had stomachaches almost every day. The teacher would send me to the school nurse, and she would send me back to class. One day, the principal, Mr. Blume, a large, plump man with a cherry-red nose, called me into his office. "That's enough," he said in his gruff voice. "Quit making up stories that your stomach hurts. There is nothing wrong with you. Now go back to class, and I don't want you to come back to the nurse's office again."

I remember feeling sad that nobody believed me. My stomach really did hurt. I didn't understand why it hurt, but it did. I learned to keep my feelings to myself. Nobody wanted to hear how I felt.

As a teenager and into my early twenties, I continued to keep my feelings to myself. I would tell myself that it was okay and found ways to distance myself from my feelings. Zoning out, daydreaming, pretending things didn't matter were coping mechanisms for me.

Irene Owning Her Feelings

I was playing basketball after school when I experienced my first migraine. I was sixteen. My mother had migraines regularly, and now I knew how she felt. The sunlight was my enemy. I tied a handkerchief around my forehead and covered my eyes. I hid my face in my pillow. I had to endure the pain for hours. After a night's rest, the headache usually subsided. But sometimes the effects lingered, and it would take days before I was back to normal.

As the years went by, I recognized signs that a migraine was about to begin. My vision in one eye would be blurred. At that point I had about a half hour before the onset of the headache. If I was able to take medication before it began, I could control the pain. For years, this became a way of life for me, and I often had migraines once or twice a month.

I began to notice a pattern. If I was in upset, I developed a migraine a day or two later. When I was in a major depression, I had migraines on a daily basis.

I began to process my feelings, feelings that I didn't even know I had. Some of them went back to childhood. I had buried them deep inside me, and I realized I had been really good at that. I was so good, I had fooled myself. When I was honest with myself and owned my feelings, I found the window out of depression and my migraines stopped. That was twelve years ago, and I can't remember the last time I had a migraine.

Healing Actions

Self-Discovery Journal

Continue writing in your self-discovery journal. Remember to become present with yourself. Don't filter or censor your thoughts or feelings. Let them flow directly from your heart, through your hand, and onto the page. The level of healing you receive from this exercise is equal to your intention and willingness to dig deep.

Tool 3: Meditation

Develop a sacred space, an altar, a corner of a room, a place where you can go to be with yourself: a place of meditation, communion, and contemplation. This is a place where you know you will not be disturbed. Set your boundaries. Let your family know that when you are in this place, you are not to be disturbed and to honor your privacy. You may want to create a sign for your door or use some other signal to let them know that this is your private time and space.

Creating this space will begin to set the energy for it. You will find that as you use your sacred space, it will be easier for you to become centered, and the processes will flow more freely. Try to find at least twenty minutes a day for quiet contemplation.

Cloud Meditation

Center yourself in your loving heart. Take a deep breath in from the bottom of your soul. As you breathe out, release any tension, upsets, or discomfort from your day. Breathe in loving connection to your spiritual source. Breathe out any negative thoughts or feelings. Do this several times. Sit quietly for a few minutes just noticing your breathing. You need not do or try to change anything, simply notice.

After a few minutes, consider how you chose to respond to the people and events in your life. You don't need to try to bring anything specific up. Just allow your thoughts or feelings to become present. Scan the events of the last day or two as if you were watching a play. The main character is not you, but an actor playing you. When something happens or someone says something to this actor, how does the actor respond? Is it in a loving way? Is anger or another emotion being displayed? You are the director of this play. Would you like to rewrite the script and have a different response? Go ahead, this is your play. Do you notice your actor engaging in any self-destructive or self-defeating behaviors? Write a new script and "reshoot" the scene.

After a few minutes, bring your awareness back to your heart center. From this place send loving thoughts and prayers to all of the actors in your play. Now bring your awareness back into the room. Move your fingers and toes. When you are ready, open your eyes.

Inner Reflections

What are some of your favorite methods for zoning out or avoiding your feelings? What are the real costs of continuing these behaviors? What would you like to change? What would you have to let go?

Looking back at the choice diagram. Are you moving up, down, or are you stuck? What direction would you like to go? Can you envision yourself in "Living Loving"?

You can write about what comes up for you in a separate journal or you can meditate on these questions. Either way, do not force anything. Just allow whatever comes forward without judgment.

4

A Lifetime of Loving

The unexamined life is not worth living.

—Socrates

Choosing To Live

When my wife asked me for a separation, I was devastated. I felt lost and alone. I wondered, *Where do I go from here?* I was empty inside. Though I was not aware of it, this wasn't the first time I'd had these feelings. I had built my life around someone else's expectations, hopes, and dreams. I had forgotten who I was, particularly all of my positive qualities.

In the quote above, Socrates makes an astute observation. We would amend it slightly to read, "An unexamined life lacks awareness and may lead to unintended consequences." It is important to affirm the positive as well as our current suffering. It's easy to get caught up in our problems and negative issues, thereby losing perspective of the complete picture.

Our lives and relationships contain positive aspects as well as challenges. When we are upset or feeling down, it is often difficult to remember those positive aspects. When we make an assessment of our lives, it is important to affirm the positive experiences and relationships as well as these we perceive as negative. These positive memories can become our guiding light out of our personal tornados.

Ultimately, we are purging ourselves of the toxic energy we have been carrying inside ourselves, so that we can embrace a positive life moving forward. This includes bringing closure to past relationships, finding blessings, and acknowledging the gifts and lessons learned.

We are asking you to make an honest assessment of the events and relationships in your life and to look at them in a different light, perhaps in a way you have never thought of before. Maybe all of these events were opportunities in disguise. How can you grow from your adversities? How can you learn from your adversaries? Often these events give us our greatest opportunities to become wiser and more compassionate. They can increase our ability to connect with others at a deeper, more loving level.

Here is where your choices lie. You may feel that the things that have happened to you were not your fault or that you had no other choice in the decisions you made, but you always have the choice of your attitude. After all, who is being hurt when you hold onto these less than loving memories? You can choose to view your life as a learning and growing opportunity, or you can play the role of the victim. This is *your* choice. You may not be able to control the circumstances of your life, but you can choose your attitude.

The degree to which you are not in alignment with the way things really are is the degree that you will be unhappy, upset, or feel like a victim. When you say, "I'm upset because ..." you are really acknowledging your inability to see, or your unwillingness to accept, the reality of your life. Understand that acceptance is not the same as agreement. We may not wish to be in the situation we are in, but when we are able to see exactly where we are, right here and now, we are better prepared to make effective, positive changes in our lives.

You will undoubtedly be more successful at affecting change if you are not coming from a place of upset or anger. When you are in distress, you are not in touch with the highest parts of yourself. You are not in your loving self. Think about it from another perspective. Are you more or less open to hearing someone else's point of view when they are agitated or when they are calm and centered? This includes your own self-talk!

If you are holding onto your past story, this may be affecting your ability to feel and function in the present and to plan for your future. When looking for opportunities to heal yourself, be aware of support groups that can keep you stuck. Look instead for groups that process emotions up and out. Some groups tend to stay in victim consciousness and support one another by retelling the stories of events from the mental level only.

Each loss is unique. How everyone processes his or her loss is unique. Everyone must find their own way to move forward along their journey through grief, if they choose. When you hold onto the past you limit your ability to experience joy and love. Unresolved heartache colors your view of the world making everything appear negative.

> It may be hard for an egg to turn into a bird: it would be a jolly sight harder for it to learn to fly while remaining an egg. We are like eggs at present. And you cannot go on indefinitely being just an ordinary, decent egg. We must be hatched or go bad.
>
> —C. S. Lewis

How do you see the world? Do you choose to see the pain and suffering that exists in everyone, or do you choose to look beyond the suffering and see the loving, eternal soul that exists in everyone's hearts? Our job is to release the suffering and embrace the loving. What am I holding onto in thought, action, or deed that no longer serves my highest good?

A life without challenges would be boring. We went to the supermarket and picked up a few things. How exciting! Let me see. I think I'll have a box of self-doubt, a package of anger, and can I get loathing by the ounce or do I need to buy the whole pound?

Are you laughing or frowning? Oh, you think that these are negative things? You *judge* them as bad? What if it were true that they were neither good nor bad, only challenges? And what if it were also true that viewing them from a neutral point of view makes it a whole lot easier to handle them? We all have a few of these items in our shopping carts, don't we? And this point of view changes them from problems to challenges. Your life becomes a life to be lived, full of interesting challenges, rather than simply problems to be solved.

Remember the movie *The Stepford Wives*? It presented a very unrealistic view of perfection. Nothing ever went wrong. What an absolutely boring and pointless life. It is in these perceived imperfections, problems, and challenges that we discover an interesting life. We find clues to our true natures and how we can be of service. What unique gifts, talents, and challenges do you have to share with the world?

A fundamental change in consciousness is that there is nothing to be added. It is a process of discovering, uncovering, and expressing what already is.

Men and Women Process Differently

What works for one person may not work for another. I process information through the mental realm first, before I get to the emotional. Irene is a touchy-feely person, so there are some exercises that she enjoys more than I do. She likes to talk things out; I like to think things through. Just because a man isn't talking a lot doesn't mean he isn't doing the work. We learned this the hard way—through personal experience.

Where does someone learn the skill of communicating? When you're growing up, it's usually your parents who teach you how to talk. Your vocabulary increases over time as you listen to others and become exposed to more people and more conversations. The most common words and phrases are easily learned; and even those words identified as "not nice words" can be repeated by children without their understanding what they are saying. As adults we carry our childhood-learned patterns of communicating into our relationships, often without the benefit of having upgraded our communications toolbox. We continue to utilize old communication techniques that we often learned from watching how our parents processed their issues.

In the past, Irene's method of communicating included avoiding any and all conflicts.

I would cry very easily and leave the scene by going into another room to be alone. I grew up walking on eggshells, afraid to bring attention to myself, afraid to upset others, and unwilling to deal with uncomfortable situations. My father gave me the nickname crybaby, and it was easy for me to live up to this name. Everyone expected it.

I continued to use these same methods of communicating and processing in my first marriage. I held my feelings in. I didn't express how I felt. I cried and left the room whenever there was a disagreement. I didn't know how to do it differently. I didn't know I had a choice.

In our relationship, Bill and I have developed our own unique style of communicating. But in order to do this, we had to first become aware of how we had been handling situations and why that wasn't working.

After Shannon died, it was as if we sleepwalked through the weeks and months that followed. Bill went to work every morning, and when he returned home he isolated himself in front of the computer or television. Harboring anger and bitterness, he fell deeper into the black void of emotional unavailability.

I didn't know how to share with him what I was going through. I assumed he felt like I did, but when he didn't express his feelings, I felt anger growing inside me. I didn't want to be the only one grieving. I found myself judging him for not grieving the "right" way. We grew further apart, unresolved issues festering inside both of us.

A few years later, Irene fell into a deep depression, and every day seemed like a blur. There were no highs or recognizable lows; her mood was consistently low and lifeless. She walked around like a zombie, putting one foot in front of the other, a shell of existence. She didn't have to think about anything—didn't want to think. Every day seemed like a copy of the previous day.

We didn't know how to process our heartache, so we let it consume us. It felt like we had been swept up into the tornado of life.

No one ever taught us the tools and techniques to navigate through heartache. Our only experience had been processing previous heartaches the best way we knew how. If we had known better, we would have done things differently.

We are all different in how we learn and process. There isn't one right way to move from heartache to happiness. That is why we share a variety of exercises. If one exercise doesn't work as well as you thought it might, put it aside. Maybe the next exercise will be more effective.

Why Me?

Why, oh, why me? Why not someone else or anyone else? *Why* is ultimately an unproductive question that pulls us deeper into the tornado and away from moving into a more loving life. Unless you are omniscient, you will never know the answer to most why questions. It doesn't change where you are and the issues you have to deal with. Why questions are a distraction. They give you an excuse to be a victim of your own story. Life has handed you these lessons, and you can choose to heal or stay stuck in your story. You don't heal at the story level. A more useful and healing frame of mind would be to ask the question, what can I learn from this experience? When you learn that lesson, you can begin to see the gift in the experience.

Meditation

Gather a few of your old photographs: maybe some of you growing up, perhaps a few of your parents and other relatives, mementos and keepsakes that remind you of various periods of your life, souvenirs from special trips, or gifts from someone special. Go to your sacred space and center yourself in your loving heart. Light a candle or fill the room with gentle music. Close your eyes and take a deep breath from the bottom of your soul. As you breathe out, release any tension, upsets, or discomfort from your day. Breathe in loving connection to your spiritual source. Breathe out any negative thoughts or feelings. Do this several times. Sit quietly for a few minutes just noticing your breathing. Now open your eyes and take a few moments to hold and look at each object you have gathered. Focus only on one object at a time. Maybe you remember when a picture was taken, or actually posing for it. Or maybe you have fond memories of a trip and when you purchased a certain souvenir. There may be some feelings of sadness or upset; allow them to become present. Don't judge your feelings, just be aware of anything that surfaces. Let the objects take you back in time, and remember what you felt like then. Continue to go through all of the objects in this manner, taking as long as you need to complete this process.

The Life Review Chart

Did anyone ever take a course in school called, "How to handle heartache"? It's more likely we learned by experience, often early in life and not very well.

In this next exercise, you will have an opportunity to look at all the major events in your life. Take a look at Bill's example of the life review chart, entitled, "A Lifetime of Loving" on page 48. On the far left side of the chart, Bill has written his birth year. His first memory, bunny costume, is indicated as a positive event. Lines extending above the time line indicate positive experiences, lines below are negative. The length of the line indicates the intensity of the event when it occurred. On the far right side of the chart is the most recent significant event Bill remembers. Don't worry if you don't understand the labels of Bill's events. The example is Bill's exercise, and the titles only need to have meaning to him. You will have the opportunity to write titles that mean something to you.

The Life Review Instructions

Go to your sacred place. Take out a piece of paper and create your own life review chart. Take a few minutes just to be with yourself. Take a few deep, cleansing breaths. Write your name on the top of the chart. On the far left side of the chart, write your birth year. What is your first memory? Write it down near the left side of the chart; give it a title and a date. Don't worry about being perfect or getting the dates exactly right. You can always go back and make adjustments. This is a work in progress. Title and date all of the other significant events in your life that rise in your memory, both positive and negative. You may begin with the most significant and obvious events, such as births, deaths, marriages, etc., but don't censor yourself. If something comes up, write it down. If you have remembered it, it has some sort of energy attached to it. At this point you don't necessarily know how it is attached or where that energy will lead.

We suggest you come back to this chart several times and add to it as things come forward.

Tool 4: A Lifetime of Loving

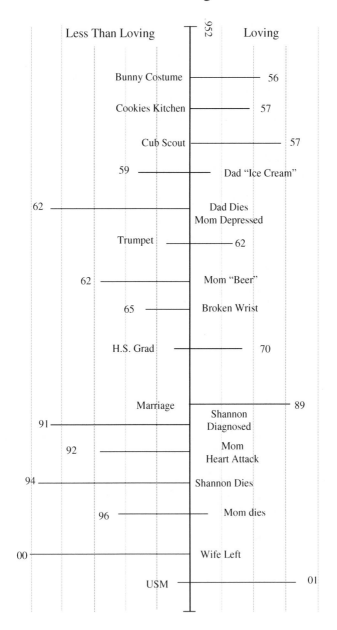

48

Tool 5: Free-Form Writing

Six procedures for free-form writing:

- Begin a regular practice.
- Create a sacred place.
- Put pen or pencil to paper.
- Set an intention.
- Write until you are out of your mind.
- Don't go back; burn it.

A regular practice of free-form writing can be an effective tool for moving through blocks and releasing negative energy buried within your consciousness. It is also a great way to relieve the mind of clutter, a kind of mental download.

The procedure should be done with pencil or pen and paper. The tactile connection of your consciousness through your hand to the pen and to the paper is important. There is a direct pathway from your heart to your fingertips. Set aside a specific amount of time at regular intervals to help build the energy. For example, twenty minutes three times a week for one month, or thirty minutes a day for ten days. You can also designate a number of pages to do in each session. The number isn't as important as the regularity and commitment. Pick a place that is quiet and where you won't be interrupted. You might wish to light a candle to help create a sacred space.

We work with free-form writing in two basic ways. One way is to clear our minds of the clutter of thoughts we have. The other is when we are working with a specific challenge or issue. Either way, write an intention at the top of the page. If you are using this procedure to clear the mind, you might write something like, "My intention for this process is to clear my mind so that I can be a clear channel to create." If you are working with a particular issue, use something like, "My intention for this session is to release all of the anger and upset I have about my mother that is available to me at this time, for the highest good of all concerned."

Begin writing whatever comes to your mind without censoring, analyzing, or controlling. Keep your pen moving. If your mind changes thoughts in the middle of a sentence, go with it. It doesn't need to make sense. Just keep writing. If nothing come to your mind, you can write, "I can't think of anything to write," or "This is a fine pen," or anything else. Just keep writing.

Do not go back and reread anything you have written. The purpose of this exercise is to get the thoughts out of your head, onto the page, and out of your energy field. Reading what you wrote will put that energy right back into your mind. Tear the pages up and throw them away. If the session was particularly emotional or toxic, it could be helpful to burn your pages in a ceremony. As the pages burn you could say something like, "I release these emotions and this energy into the flames so that I may be free."

When this process is used for mind clearing, really good ideas often come out and onto the page. If this is the case, simply transcribe the great ideas into another notebook specifically for that purpose.

Healing Actions

Self-Discovery Journal

Continue writing in your self-discovery journal. Remember to be present with yourself. Don't filter or censor your thoughts or feelings. Let them flow directly from your heart, through your hand, and onto the page.

Inner Reflections

What would it mean to you if you were able to detach from the emotions of a situation and view that situation as if through the eyes of a reporter?

What direction do you think you are facing most of the time, in the direction of Living Loving or of Loss & Pain?

What would it mean to you if you were able to experience more loving in your life? Are you able to give more of this to yourself? What is your intention for your life direction?

You can write about what comes up in a separate journal or you can focus on these questions in meditation. Either way, do not force anything. Just allow whatever comes forward without judgment.

5

Commitment to Self

When we align our thoughts, emotions, and actions with the highest part of ourselves, we are filled with enthusiasm, purpose, and meaning. Life is rich and full. We have no thoughts of bitterness. We have no memory of fear. We are joyously and intimately engaged with our world. This is the experience of authentic power.

—Gary Zukav, cofounder
The Seat of the Soul Institute

Life Review Awareness

Take a look at each of the events on your life review chart. Sit with them; breathe into them. Allow yourself to connect with the times and places. What feelings come up around the first event? Write them down. Do the same for each event. Look at your list of feelings. Do you see a pattern emerging?

Identify the patterns. There may be more than one. Our experiences and feelings can reveal one or more of our core spiritual lessons. Until we work with and heal these issues, they will keep reappearing in our lives, in varying degrees.

For example, as you look at the events on your life review chart, there may not appear to be any patterns. But when you look at feelings associated with these experiences, you may find a pattern of abandonment. At an unconscious level, you may be inviting this experience into your life until you become aware of it and heal it.

Feelings and Patterns

You will be deepening your healing with your life review chart. You will have an opportunity to access buried feelings associated with each event, and bring them up and out.

You've taken a look at your lifetime of significant life events. Now you will focus on one individual with whom you have had a significant relationship.

Preparing Your Relationship Review

Look at the example on page 56. Bill has chosen his mother as his relationship project. The year Bill was born is noted on the left side of the chart. His first significant event with his mother was in 1956, when she made him a bunny costume for Halloween. It is a happy memory, so the line indicating its significance is above the loving line.

In 1962, his father dies. Compounding this event, his mother stops baking and engaging in the lives of her three children, slowly moving into depression. She also takes a full-time job outside the home. After doing his relationship review, Bill realized he had felt abandoned by both his father and mother. He felt his mother had become emotionally unavailable to him.

Once again, it doesn't matter that the events are described in detail for anyone other than the person creating the chart.

Go to your sacred space. Take out a piece of paper and create your own relationship review. Take a few minutes just to be with yourself. Take a few cleansing breaths. Write your name on the right side of the chart. You need to choose one relationship in your life to work with at this time, so look at your life review chart. Which person is most present in your feelings? Write the person's name you have chosen to work with in the middle of your chart. If you feel resistance to working with someone on your life review chart, he or she may be the perfect person for you to work with for the maximum amount of healing. For a deeper level of healing, complete the relationship meditation on page 55 before preparing your relationship review.

Indicate the year you met the person on the left side of the chart. This is the beginning of your timeline. Enter today's date on the right edge of the chart. Enter the dates of all significant events with this person. If you do not know the exact date, that's okay. Enter positive events above the line and negative events below the line. Don't be too quick to judge an event you remember as insignificant. It might have appeared insignificant at the time it occurred, but if you remember it, it must have had some importance.

Relationship Meditation

Gather photographs and mementos that pertain to the person you have chosen for your relationship review and place them in your sacred space. Center yourself in your loving heart. Light a candle and fill the room with gentle music. Bring an extra chair into the room and place it across from where you are sitting. Close your eyes and take a deep breath, in from the bottom of your soul. As you breathe out, release any tension, upsets, or discomfort. Breathe in loving connection to your spiritual source. Breathe out any negative thoughts or feelings. Do this several times. Sit quietly for a few minutes just noticing your breathing. Say to yourself, "I surround, fill, and protect myself with love and white light."

With your eyes still closed, bring forward the individual you have chosen for your relationship review. Imagine him or her sitting across from you, surrounded by all of the pictures and mementos you have brought into this sacred space. See his features clearly, beginning with the top of his head and working your way down his face. See him smiling at you, looking peaceful and content. Now with your eyes still closed, consider the pictures and mementos, one at a time, and recall specific events you had with the individual over the years. Allow yourself to feel what it was like in the moment. Don't judge the feelings; just allow yourself to be present with them. Notice the feelings that were pleasant and those that weren't so pleasant. If emotion comes up, that's okay. Simply let it be.

When you feel complete, lovingly express your gratitude to the individual for joining you to assist with this process.

Then wiggle your toes, shake your hands, and open your eyes. Allow yourself a few minutes of silent time to reflect on the process.

Tool 6: Relationship Review

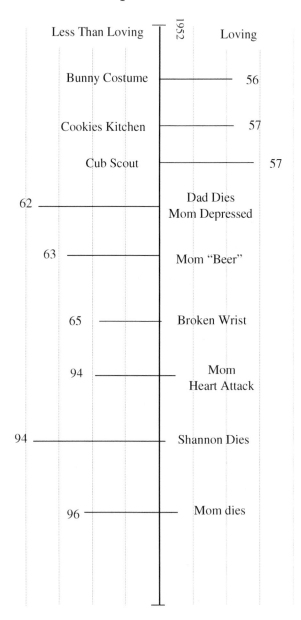

Feelings Mapping

It is important to dig deep into feelings. You want to examine and release the negative feelings you are holding onto. Get out of your head (and your thoughts), access your feelings, and bring them forward.

For a deeper cut, take some of the major events from your relationship review chart and create a feelings map on a separate piece of paper. (See Bill's example on the following page.) With each of these major events, sit back and remember what you felt at the time. What were some of the feelings and judgments you experienced? Write down these feelings as arms off each experience.

These are probably some of the core issues you have been carrying around most of your life. It is important to uncover these feelings and judgments. We will continue to work with them as we move through more exercises in this book.

EXAMPLE

Feelings Map   Person: _____ Mom _____

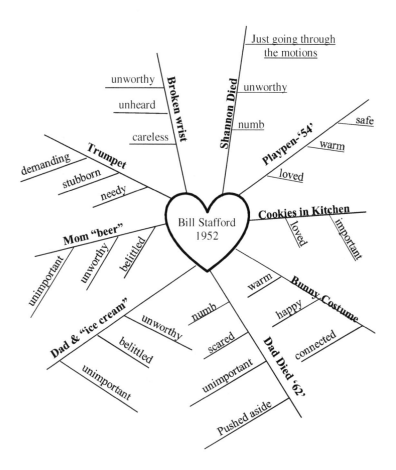

Reframing Issues as Blessings

It was the worst thing that ever happened to me.

It was the best thing that ever happened to me.

These two statements actually describe the same event, something that actually happened to me. How can these two opposite statements be true at the same time? When my wife left me, I thought it was the worst thing that had ever happened to me. It was extremely painful. It cracked me open in a way I never could have imagined. I was ready.

But ready for what? Because of that event, I began a quest to discover what could heal those things inside me that were so uncomfortable and painful. I was finally willing to accept life the way it was. I had thought I was happy before, but I'd been unaware of the nagging pain, frustration, and mild depression I had been living with. It was the highest level of living I could achieve at the time. I didn't know there could be more. If my wife hadn't left me, I might never have discovered how much more there could be to life. And I would have lived a somewhat happy existence.

What I discovered was so much more than I had imagined. I didn't have to hold onto past hurts and pains. I learned the tools to set myself free. In looking back, separating from Irene was the best thing that ever happened to me. What I found were the tools and the ability to live in higher levels of happiness, joy, and loving.

This is the essence of a tool I call, reframing your issues as blessings. Whatever experience you've gone through or are going through, you can learn a lesson from it. You can take something from it to help you grow and become even more compassionate, loving, or accepting of your circumstances. It is a new way to view the world.

The world, the people, and the events of our lives: none of them are against us. It really isn't us against the world. Everything is for us in some way. It is our job, our responsibility, and opportunity to discover how we can use the events in our lives to grow, to reach higher levels of consciousness and loving.

Reframing Worksheet Instructions

The purpose of this exercise is to write a reframe for each event listed on your relationship review chart. Bill remembered an incident he had with his mother when he was a child. In his relationship review chart on page 56, he labeled it "Mom and Beer." He still felt some negative energy when he remembers this event, so he chose to take it deeper and find another way to hold this experience. On his reframing worksheet on page 61, he has titled the event "The Beer," and he wrote how he felt when the event occurred and the reframe for it.

Tool 7: The Reframing Worksheet

Complete the worksheet below with each event from your relationship review chart. Write a reframe using the following format.

Example: The Beer

How I took it in: *I felt belittled, unsafe, like I was doing something wrong, a bad person*

The greater truth (reframe): *Her reaction wasn't about me. She was afraid and upset (with herself). She probably felt trapped and alone, unable to find joy for herself*

How I took it in: *I felt unworthy of being loved*

The greater truth (reframe): *I was only nine years old. I had recently lost my father and was afraid that my mother would abandon me too. I know now how overwhelmed with grief my mother felt at that time. Her reaction was triggered by her own pain and suffering and had nothing to do with me.*

Event Title: _____

How I took it in:

The greater truth (reframe):

As you reflect on your own reframing worksheet, do you notice any patterns?

In the past, how you processed events may have served a purpose for you, but today you have an opportunity to update how you respond and react to events in your life from a different perspective.

Holding onto fear, shame, guilt, and self-judgment does not serve any of us in moving forward.

Narrative from a Past Workshop

Betsy: From the worksheet I realized that I was getting upset at other people for the choices I made. I felt trapped and envious of others.

I have a friend, and unlike me, she doesn't have a lot of the fears that I have, so she is always traveling. She is constantly going to exciting places and doing these things that I would just love to do, but either I don't have the money, someone to go with, or I'm too fearful. I have caught myself so often getting really upset when I hear she is going someplace. In the past I was getting obsessed with judging her and wondering why I couldn't have some of what she had. I'm trying not to get so caught up in comparing myself and just being grateful for what I do have, but I would like to have some of what she has in my life too. I think it's natural to want to have fun and go on vacations and do fun things. So when she called me the other night and said she wouldn't be available, right away my reaction was, here we go again. She gets to have fun and I get to work an extra job. That's kind of how my life has been, but it has been choices I have made too.

I would like to become more content with my life. My life has been out of balance tremendously, both in responsibility and sadness, and not a lot of fun.

Irene: And that's really the key, finding balance. For me, most of my life it was always black and white, right and wrong, this side or that side. After becoming aware of my patterns, taking personal responsibility, I realized—wait a minute, I have more choices. There is an in between, and it doesn't have to be all work, work, work, and no fun. I realized I was the only one holding myself back from allowing more joy into my life.

Healing Actions

Self-Discovery Journal

Continue writing in your self-discovery journal. Remember to become present with yourself. Don't filter or censor your thoughts or feelings, just let them flow directly from your heart, through your hand, and onto the page.

The Art of the Reframe

Set aside time to practice the art of the reframe. Use the reframe worksheet exercise to bring a new level of awareness and acceptance to any issue that comes up. The more you use this tool, the easier it will become to let go of negative thought patterns that do not allow you to move into a more positive, self-honoring life.

William W. Stafford

Meditation

Continue to develop your practice of going within and discovering yourself. Remember to set your boundaries and let your family know that you are not to be disturbed. You may want to listen to music during the meditation that reminds you of the person you have been working with in your relationship project. Before you begin, place an object that reminds you of this person in front of you at eye level. As you begin this closed eye process, hold that image in your mind's eye, concentrating on the image throughout your meditation. If you find your mind wandering, do not judge yourself, just begin the process again. You will find that the more you practice meditating, the easier it will become.

6

I Was Never Enough

We can start to alleviate suffering by looking into the eyes of a family member or friend and telling them something kind and encouraging. And when we come together to do this in groups, life becomes altogether a more joyful, peaceful enterprise.

—Joan Borysenko, author of *Fire in the Soul:
A New Psychology of Spiritual Optimism*

Unmet Expectations

People often want to put a cap on their feelings. They may say something like, "It's over and done with, time to move on. No use crying over spilled milk." This is like putting on a Band-Aid. It covers up the wound, but the wound is still there. The hurt feelings are still in us, buried under the surface. All of these feelings, our feelings, want to be healed and set free. We will carry these around with us as unconscious, unresolved issues until we deal with them. Unresolved issues are like magnets. They attract people and events into our lives that help to get our attention, to bring our awareness to all of the inner wounds we are carrying around with us. Add to this the other unresolved issues in our lives, and you can see that there are probably a lot of conflicting pain vying for our attention. It can become exhausting. Our inner selves really want us to be free and clear. They will go to any lengths to get our attention so that we have the opportunity to heal our inner conflicts. Our higher selves are constantly encouraging us to move in the direction of clearing our issues and living a life of joy and loving. Our inner selves have our best and highest interests at heart.

Our suffering is the price we pay for our resistance. We will attract into our lives things that bring these issues to the surface until we heal them. It just is. Instead of fighting, resisting, or pushing them back down using our habitual ways of avoiding our feelings, adopt a way to gently and lovingly release those feelings that no longer serve your highest good.

Woulda, Shoulda, Coulda

Find a quiet place. Center yourself in your heart and answer the following questions. Alternate between the three questions and the pronouns (I, you, and we) as they come up. Do not censor yourself. There are no right or wrong answers, or a specific order to this exercise. Keep going until you feel complete, and then do ten more. Tune in and listen to all of your inner voices. They all want to be heard. Begin each sentence with the name of the person you are working with.

Example: Dad, I should have listened to you more.

Dad, I shouldn't have yelled at you that night.

Dad, I wish we could have been better friends.

Dad, you should have thought about the consequences of your actions.

Dad, you could have been there for me when I needed someone to just listen.

Dad, we should have spent more time together.

Dad, we could have had a more loving relationship.

Note: In the example, "I shouldn't have yelled at you that night," it isn't important that anyone but you know what night you are talking about. Also, the "shouldn't" example is naturally followed by the "I wish we could have" example. The order of the statements isn't important. Let it flow naturally. Just make sure you cover all of them.

Saying the person's name each time helps to anchor your connection with that person during this exercise. On the woulda, shoulda, coulda worksheet, write the name of the person you are working with from your relationship review. Then write the statements, beginning with the person's name. When you are finished, read them out loud to yourself.

Tool 8: Woulda, Shoulda, Coulda

Person's Name: _____

(Person's name followed by I, you, or we) should have: …

(Person's name followed by I, you, or we) should not have: …

(Person's name) I wish (I, you, or we) would have: …

(Person's name) I wish (I, you, or we) wouldn't have: …

(Person's name followed by I, you, or we) could have: …

Guilt and Shame

One of the ways we hide our true feelings is by making ourselves feel guilty and shameful. No one can do this to us; we do it to ourselves. Guilt and shame are often linked to unworthiness, not being good enough, and are actually judgments that you place on yourself. If you believe you are guilty or unworthy, if you believe you aren't good enough, then you don't have to take responsibility for how you feel at a deeper level. In essence, there are buried feelings deeper than the guilt and shame. Until you are willing to release the guilt and shame, release the judgments of yourself, you will not be able to access and release the hurt feelings underneath.

On a separate piece of paper make a list of the things you are sorry you did, sorry you said, or sorry you didn't say. (Refer to your woulda, shoulda, coulda worksheet)

Projections and Your Shadow Self

There's always something! Most people probably think of this in a bad way. They have the habit of thinking in a negative way or with a victim mentality. The world is full of whatever you are looking for. The world is a magnificent place. The universe is neutral. It will give you whatever you are looking for. Are you looking for peace, love, hope, and connection, or fear, separation, and anger? You don't have to go far to find all of these negative experiences. Most people live in the land of fear.

You see in the world what you are afraid of in yourself. Where you put your thoughts is what you will manifest in your life. You can't do it just by being positive. That's on the surface. In doing your release work, you are releasing things subconsciously.

There is a part of us we call the shadow side. There's the part of us that we are unable to see ourselves. In it are some of our darkest fears, our judgments about ourselves, the things we believe are wrong or broken in us. But that shadow side also contains some of our greatest strengths and attributes. These are the positive aspects of ourselves that we have suppressed and disowned, for whatever reason, and are unable to share with the world. Often these are our greatest gifts.

We say to ourselves, I'm not good enough to be that. Then there are the things we don't want to own, like our anger and bitterness, those impolite attributes and feelings. We have them anyway; we just don't acknowledge them. This is resistance, and resistance causes stress. It is the burden we carry all of the time. The only way we can see those attributes and feelings is when they are reflected from the outer world back to us.

Bill's Shadow

One of my core beliefs, deep down inside me, is that I am alone. There is no one like me. No one could ever understand my problems. No one could ever love me. Deep under that is the realization that I don't love myself because I can't accept myself. I stand in judgment of myself and say that I am not worthy. I can't live up to my expectations of what I think I should be. It's just more stinking thinking.

We compare ourselves to others and wish we were more like them. But what we see is only their public face, the polished image or act. Underneath the mask they have a shadow side, too, that they fiercely protect and don't want you to see. Underneath their act they have most of the same fears as you.

By nature our knowledge and perspective is limited by our actual human experiences. On the emotional side, things have happened to us that we view as challenging or unwanted. We put up blocks or barriers, and they become a part of our shadow side. Now we don't have to deal with these negative perceptions. We wonder if we could just say something different and things would change. It cannot be done, because it is in the dark part of us. We can't see it directly. The only way we can see it is when it is reflected by our outer experience, the reflection we see in others, or journaling over a period of time.

To heal you must acknowledge the existence of your shadow self, and courageously work with it, not work against it or ignore it. Whether you do or not, it's there anyway.

You cannot get through your blocks by denying their existence or pushing them away. They just get bigger and harder to handle. We get through our blocks by releasing the emotional stuff, the energy that we place on those things, and using them as opportunities to free ourselves from those feelings. Anytime you have an emotional upset of any kind, it is a signal that you are out of balance. Check in with yourself on all levels. Do you find yourself clenching your teeth? What does that tell you about your emotions? Are you experiencing worry, anger, or upset? Are your thoughts in alignment with reality? Are you disconnecting from your divine essence?

Awareness and Compassion Meditation

Go to your sacred space, or find a place in nature where you will not be disturbed. Center yourself in your loving heart. Light a candle and fill the space with gentle music. Close your eyes and take a deep breath from the bottom of your soul. As you breathe out, release any tension, upset, or discomfort from your day. Breathe in loving connection to your spiritual source. Breathe out any negative thoughts or feelings. Do this several times. Sit quietly for a few minutes just noticing your breathing. Say to yourself, "I surround, fill, and protect myself with love and white light."

Recall a time when you felt guilt, shame, or that you were not good enough. Imagine yourself sitting on top of a cloud looking down at the scene. Watch yourself interacting with the other characters in the scene. Notice your actions, your response, your participation. Notice what feelings are present as you watch this scene and where in your body they are located. Allow yourself to feel these feelings fully. You now have a choice. You can choose to release these negative feelings once and for all.

Send a bright white light streaming down from the cloud you are on and shine it on all the characters in the scene. Feel the warmth of the light and notice the peaceful expressions of the characters. As you release guilt and shame, the feeling of unworthiness, the judgments you placed on yourself and others, the light grows brighter and brighter. Peace and loving energy now fill the space where the negative feelings were stored. Allow yourself a few minutes to sit with these new feelings of peace and love, as they grow stronger and stronger.

When you feel complete, lovingly express your gratitude to your spiritual source for joining you to assist with this process.

Then wiggle your toes, shake your hands, and open your eyes. Allow yourself a few minutes of silent time to reflect on the process.

Affirmations

Affirmations are a powerful tool you can use to counteract the constant barrage of negative messages that come at us. All of this negative input can be called our background noise. No matter how hard we try or how little we pay attention to the noise, some of it filters into our subconscious internal programming. We begin to believe these negative images of ourselves.

Affirmations are our noise-canceling program. They are most effective when we use them to counteract the deep-seated negative messages we have internalized; the negative thoughts and feelings we believe about ourselves.

There is an old story of a Cherokee chief who told his grandson about a battle that goes on inside people.

"The battle is between two wolves," he said. "One is evil. It is anger, envy, sorrow, regret, greed, arrogance, self-pity, guilt, resentment, inferiority, lies, false pride, superiority, and ego. The other is good. It is peace, love, hope, serenity, humility, kindness, joy, benevolence, empathy, generosity, truth, compassion, and faith."

The grandson thought about this for a minute and asked, "Grandfather, which wolf wins?"

The old Cherokee chief replied, "The one you feed."

One of our clients recalled the constant message from her father—"You'll never find anyone who will love you. Men will always disappoint you and leave you." It doesn't matter whether this is what he actually said. It only matters that this is the message she heard. Not surprisingly, she is single and all of her relationships have been disappointing and have ended badly. It was not until she dug deep inside and recognized the pattern that it finally clicked for her. When she was able to recognize the pattern and its origin, she could then take steps to release it.

Every thought we have is attached to an emotion. Our negative emotions and upsets are a result of negative thoughts. These thoughts are based on our limited interpretations of reality or on our attachment to believing our view is right. Whenever we are in upset, it is a clear indication that what we believe to be true is in conflict with reality.

Like attracts like. The more we think of our lives as a problem to be solved, the more we create negative thoughts. Negative thought patterns become our habits. It is so easy to fall into this pattern of thinking, we don't even notice it. Before we realize it we have an overactive inner critic. Human beings are creatures of habit. What we are thinking today is probably the same as what we thought yesterday and the day before. We become like a well-worn record, and the grooves are very deep.

Affirmations are a way to overwrite our habitual negative thinking with positive, loving patterns of thought. More positive thinking leads to a more positive emotional outlook and attracts more happiness, joy, and loving. What we think about all day we become. It takes about thirty days of consistent practice to change a behavior.

An affirmation is stated in the positive with action words, as if it is already happening.

It is more powerful if energized, stated out loud with enthusiasm, and stated regularly, every day.

Example 1: I am a gentle and caring man giving and receiving love freely.

Example 2: I am a loving and compassionate woman, authentically expressing myself with others.

Bill's Affirmation

"I am a magnificent, accepting, gentle man sharing my passionate heart with you."

This is the affirmation I developed when I was going through a healing seminar. Notice the key adjectives here: magnificent, accepting, and gentle. These three words have deep meaning for me. They are the words I came up with to counteract three of my core negative beliefs about myself. For a long time I believed I was worthless. The opposite of worthless for me is *magnificent.* It doesn't matter what anyone else thinks; for me, the opposite of worthless is magnificent. These two words are linked for me. One of them is the bottom of the tornado and the other rides high on top of it.

Accepting is the opposite of pushing away or judging others in a harsh manner. I held the belief that if I pushed everyone out of my life, my pain would go away, so I wanted to affirm that I was accepting. I also recognize that I nurtured a lot of anger deep inside me, anger that no longer served me. The counter to anger, for me, was *gentle.*

This became the core of my affirmation: magnificent, accepting, and gentle. Since I recognized that I was hiding, afraid to have my heart hurt again, I wanted to learn to be more open to sharing. This is how I wanted to show up in the outside world, sharing my loving heart. I wanted to give and receive more love.

As you can see in my example, the first three core words in my affirmation are internal. Magnificent, accepting, and gentle were three qualities I wanted more of in myself. The second half of the affirmation is about how I wanted to demonstrate these qualities, and myself, in the world.

This became my affirmation, one I've used for many years. I've said this affirmation over and over to myself so many times, it has more power for me than the negative messages I've heard most of my life. In fact, this affirmation has become so powerful for me, all I have to do is say the word *magnificent* and I feel a shift inside.

Tool 9: Affirmation Worksheet

Look back over the work you have done, including your feelings map. What are the key feeling words that sting the most, the words someone has said to you or that you have said to yourself? These may reflect some of your core issues and the negative feelings you have about yourself that you've held inside for most of your life.

Pick out three words that seem to have the most energy for you and write them in the space below under *Negative Feelings*. Then write what you see as the opposite positive quality.

NEGATIVE FEELINGS   THE OPPOSITE

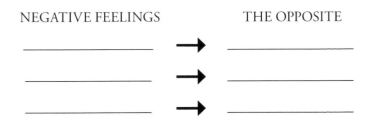

These new positive words form the core of your affirmation: the positive qualities you would like to bring forward in yourself.

Next, how are you holding yourself back? For example: hiding. What is a more positive way you could show up for yourself? For example: sharing. Write these in the spaces below.

NEGATIVE ACTION   THE OPPOSITE

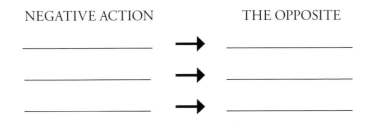

Now comes the fun part. You have created the key words that you will use to begin to cancel the negative noise inside your head. You just need to play with them until you come up with a positive affirmation that resonates deep inside you. A powerful affirmation may feel uncomfortable at first. You are releasing long-held judgments and beliefs. You still may be reluctant to let go of some of them, like an old pair of shoes or a tattered shirt that you should have thrown out years ago. Remember, your affirmation begins with the words *I am.*

My Affirmations for Living

Use the space below to refine your affirmations.

I am

I am

I am

Healing Actions

Self-Discovery Journal

Continue the practice of writing in your self-discovery journal. Remember to become present with yourself. Don't filter or censor your thoughts or feelings, just let them flow directly from your heart, through your hand, and onto the page.

Woulda, Shoulda, Coulda

Continue to work through any beliefs or feelings that you have that life should have been any way other than what it is. Use the woulda, shoulda, coulda worksheet to help to bring these feelings up and out. You can also use the worksheet as a guide to say them out loud.

Affirmations

Work through the affirmation worksheet until you have an affirmation you feel deep inside. Do not worry or stress about it, though. Your affirmation exists only to work for you. Also, these affirmations are not set in stone. Once you have an affirmation that you are comfortable with, begin to say it out loud, at least one hundred times a day.

Meditation

Continue to develop your practice of going within and discovering yourself. Remember to set your boundaries and let your family know that you are not to be disturbed. Before you begin your meditation, you may wish to review your affirmation worksheet. As you meditate, see yourself embracing the qualities of the affirmation you have created. Notice how you look and feel. Taking ownership of these new qualities, how will your life be different?

Meditation

Continue the practice of the awareness and compassion meditation from page 71.

Inner Reflections

What do you feel has been missing from your life up until now?

In general, do you focus on the positive or the negative?

How do you talk to yourself? With love and compassion, or harshly and negatively? Would you speak this way to others?

What are some of the ways you can be more loving to yourself?

7

Self-Forgiveness

Holding on to anger is like grasping a hot coal with the intent of
throwing it at someone else; you are the one who gets burned.
—Buddha

One of the most important and loving processes we can use
in healing our inner conflicts and upsets is self-forgiveness.
This is a personal journey, a journey into our own feelings, upsets,
and issues. Our inner wounds. By consistently using this process
you will be able to release your judgments, resentments, shame,
or guilt that you are holding against yourself and others.

The process of self-forgiveness has nothing to do with life events
themselves. It is about releasing the negative energy and judgments
you are holding onto that are connected with those events. Actions
in the physical world are separate and distinct from our emotional

upsets. Accepting the reality of your current state of being is one of the goals of this process.

To be clear, acceptance is not the same as giving up or giving in. It is not resignation. True acceptance allows you to begin a lively engagement with conditions as they are. Acceptance brings to you an awareness of the facts, truth, or reality of an issue, beyond the judgments.

The only thing that can really be forgiven is our judgments of our own thoughts, actions, and deeds. Our judgments keep us bound to the past. Holding on to judgments of past experiences keeps us from being able to live fully in the present. Inner peace and freedom are beyond our judgments.

What happened is in the past, and that action is complete. You need to let go of the emotional energy attached to that action. Who is being hurt by this energy? By holding on to your judgments or rightness, you are only hurting yourself. Releasing the emotional pain is where the healing is. The goal is to free yourself from the past.

Self-forgiveness is an act of self-loving. It means caring for yourself enough to let go of the people and suffering of the past, so they can no longer hurt you. This sets you free, so you are open to a more loving way of being.

The process of self-forgiveness is always about the upsets, imbalances, and suffering going on inside ourselves. It is never about anyone else or their actions. We can use our upset at someone else as an opportunity to reflect and heal unseen issues, wounds, and hurts within us. We release ourselves from the pain we are holding inside. We are clearing ourselves.

William W. Stafford

Forgiving Others

Forgiving others can be the first level of healing. Initially, this may appear as letting them off the hook. You may feel it means there are no consequences for bad behavior. But by holding on to the energy of anger or resentment, you are the one paying the price. You may have forgiven someone for whatever he or she has done, but that is only on the surface. The true healing comes when we forgive ourselves. Forgive ourselves for holding onto the energy, the feeling, or the judgment about the event or action. This is experienced in the emotional and spiritual levels of being.

> If we could read the secret history of our enemies, we should find in each man's life, sorrow and suffering enough to disarm all hostility.
> —Henry Wadsworth Longfellow

With self-forgiveness, you release your current level of thinking and the emotional upset that you are holding onto. It is not forgiving an action that anyone might have done; it has nothing to do with the action of others or what went on in our lives. It is letting go of the negative energy of judgments so that we can be free, allowing that energy to go up and out.

Negative emotional energy is a heavy burden. It weighs on our souls and saps the vitality from our lives. The sooner we can free ourselves from this burden, the sooner we can lead freer, more energetic, and loving lives.

Often it is our judgment of right and wrong that keeps us from letting go. As if somehow the other person will feel the punishment of your anger. As if it is your responsibility to punish the other person. Suffering is the price you pay for this level of thinking. We are not forgiving any action. We are forgiving ourselves for holding that energy, and releasing the judgment that is keeping us bound, preventing us from accepting our loving hearts.

This cannot be emphasized enough—your healing is not about the other person. It is not even about what happened in the physical realm. It is only about the negative energy you are holding onto. This is really the good news. It is entirely within you to heal any and all of your suffering. You do not need anyone else present, and you do not need their permission. You only need to be committed to healing yourself from the inside out.

Physical Pain

You may have heard stories of people who hold onto anger and resentment for twenty years or more, only to discover that the other person wasn't even aware of the incident.

Who was being hurt by all of that? Our habitual thinking and judgments turn into emotions, fear, anger, and resentment, and may eventually manifest in our bodies as physical illness.

"He's such a pain in the neck." Whose neck has the pain? Not his. It might be more correct to say, "When I think of him, all of these emotions come up. I don't really want to feel these feelings, but I was never taught the tools to release them, so I will manifest it as actual pain in my neck." Our emotions will go someplace—a pain in the neck, a migraine, or maybe a heart attack.

We hold onto these negative emotions or energies in different places in our bodies. Some people have chronic migraine or stomach troubles. Still others feel tension everywhere in their bodies. Have you ever had that pit feeling in your stomach? Where do you hold your tension?

You can use this information to your advantage. It can point you in the direction of healing opportunities. Your body is sending you a signal that you have an emotional issue that is not being dealt with. It is trying to get your attention.

We have been taught to take a pill for our pains. The symptom will go away for a little while, but underneath the issue is still there and growing ever larger. We continue to pile more and more issues on top, and it becomes such an overwhelming burden, we don't know where to begin or what the original issue was. Buried feelings do not stay buried. They manifest somewhere, as anger or resentment, or in the physical body as chronic pain or illness.

Compassionate Self-Forgiveness

The process of self-forgiveness is actually very simple. Sometimes we make things more difficult than they need to be because of our fears. We may be afraid of

> Compassionate self-forgiveness is loving yourself through the pain and suffering.
> —Bill Stafford

letting go of our past way of thinking or being. Who would I be without this we wonder? It's all I know. That is just the fear talking: resistance to moving forward, resistance to being seen, resistance to accepting yourself for the loving being you already are.

Forgiveness must be done in a specific way, because the energy is being released from all levels: our physical bodies, our minds, and our emotions. It opens the pathway to our souls. You have to be careful that you don't add words that turn it into a judgment. The first time, you will probably only hear the statements in your head, but as you say them over and over, they will sink deeper into the other layers of your existence. Eventually you will feel them in your heart. When you are able to feel them in your heart, then the healing really takes place.

Bill's Process

My father died when I was nine years old. I still have some energy around that event. I have judgments about how I behaved and how I expected others to behave. I know the energy is there, but I am unclear about what it is.

This is one of the great benefits of the compassionate self-forgiveness process. You don't need to know anything about the issue or what you are holding onto. That is often buried in the shadow, unseen by our thinking minds, but holding us back from fully realizing and experiencing our lives. This is not a mental process. We need to access and release the emotional energy. The thinking mind just gets in the way.

Example:

I find a comfortable spot where I won't be disturbed, set an intention to be fully with my experience, and release any judgments or negative energy I may be holding onto. I close my eyes, put my hands over my heart, and begin:

I forgive myself for judging myself as a bad son.
I forgive myself for judging myself as afraid and running away.
I forgive myself for judging my dad as abandoning me.

I forgive myself for judging my dad for dying.

I forgive myself for judging my mother as emotionally distant.

I forgive myself for judging my mom and dad as not taking care of me.

The truth of the matter is, they did the best they knew how at the time.

The truth of the matter is, I did the best I knew how at the time with the tools I had. If I'd known a better way, I would have done a better way.

The truth of the matter is, it is unreasonable to expect I would have had the tools to handle all of this at nine years old.

It is important to go with the flow of the process. As you can see by my statements, I went from myself to my dad to my mom. Follow the flow of the emotional energy, allowing it to move freely. This doesn't follow any preconceived mental logic.

The process goes on for as long as it takes. Stop when you feel complete, or when you feel the energy break and you move back into your thinking mind.

The positive truth statements are important. You can say one after each self-forgiveness statement, or you can say a few self-forgiveness statements in a row and then follow up with the positive truths. The specifics do not matter. Use whichever you feel more comfortable with as you are in the flow of the process. The positive statements are essential to the process, though. Do not skip them.

At the end, thank yourself for your courage and commitment to your healing and moving forward. For example:

I acknowledge myself for my courage to go deep within, to access my discomfort and pain and release this energy that no longer serves me. I am grateful for the level of freedom and loving I experience in my life today. I look forward to the higher levels of freedom I will experience as I continue to work my process.

The Statements

Use these statements exactly as they are written. The words in each sentence and their order are important, particularly to our subconscious mind.

I forgive myself for judging myself as _____.
I forgive myself for judging _____ as _____.
I forgive myself for judging myself for _____.
I forgive myself for judging _____ for _____.
I forgive myself for buying into the belief that _____.

The following is an alternate self-forgiveness statement. It is particularly useful for working with limiting beliefs or things you think that aren't true:

I forgive myself for buying into the belief _____.

After you say your self-forgiveness statements, it is important to follow them immediately with positive truth statements. Forgive the judgment and affirm the inner truth. The words you use are not as important as the positive regard you give yourself.

And the truth of the matter is _____.

*   *   *

The self-forgiveness process is not something you will do once and the issue will be gone. It is a tool you will use over and over. You may feel a release immediately, or it may occur over time. Do not judge the process. It takes as long as it takes. There is no timetable for healing.

You know it has been effective when it affects you at the heart level. You will know without a doubt. If you are wondering, did I do it from the heart or the head, you did it from the head. And that's great, just keep going. The process is not difficult, but it does take practice and persistence.

This is one of the most powerful tools for healing. It is letting go of past experiences we hold as negative: the judgments, anger, guilt, and shame. It is letting go of having to be right about anything. It is just *being*. When we commit to the practice of this art, it becomes an automatic program that we use anytime, and every time, we find ourselves in upset.

The release of negative emotions may bring forward an authentic experience of joy, happiness, or loving. A burst of euphoria. Allow yourself to be fully present with this experience. You are now experiencing your own divine, loving nature.

Filling Your Heart with Loving

Once you do the release work, you may feel emotionally drained. There will be an empty space where all that negative energy was. That space must and will be filled. You now have a choice over what is going to fill that void. You can take back in the energies of fear, or you can fill the space with love or gratitude. It is entirely up to you. We suggest a daily practice of positive affirmations, gratitudes, or self-loving rituals.

This is a wonderful time to begin a gratitude journal. Write at least three things you are grateful for each day, possibly as your last exercise each day before you go to bed. You have been releasing negative energy, and you want to replace it with positive energy. The more you fill yourself with positive energy, the higher your emotional energy will rise. When you move to a higher energy level, you can look down at some of your issues or problems and, from that perspective, find solutions. This is a lifelong process.

End of the Beginning

This has been an introduction to self-forgiveness as a lifetime practice. We suggest you integrate it into your daily life. When a judgment comes up, who is being served by it? Who is being hurt by the judgment? I am. And so I forgive myself for holding onto this negative energy. I don't want to live with it inside me any longer. I want to be free of it. And the truth of the matter is, whatever I am holding onto keeps me from fully experiencing all of the loving in the world that is available to me. I did the best I knew at the time with the information I had, or my father did the best he knew how to do, or my mother, or whoever. The truth of the matter is, I am a loving divine light and I have many fine attributes. I do not need to focus on things that I perceive as negative.

Tool 10: Self-Forgiveness Worksheet

The order of the self-forgiveness statements is only a suggestion. The order is not important, but it is important to use all of them. Use each statement as many times as necessary until you feel complete. Use more paper as needed. Say your self-forgiveness out loud. It is particularly powerful when you say it while looking in a mirror.

I forgive myself for judging myself as _____.
And the truth of the matter is _____.

I forgive myself for judging _____ as (acting) _____.
And the truth of the matter is _____.

I forgive myself for judging myself for _____.
And the truth of the matter is _____.

I forgive myself for judging _____ for (acting as) _____.
And the truth of the matter is _____.

I forgive myself for buying into the belief that _____.
And the truth of the matter is _____.

Gratitude

When we are in the middle of a traumatic event or swirling in its aftermath, we just want it to stop. Often we are not only going through the physical motions, but also repressing the feelings that are swirling inside us. The furthest thing from our minds is finding the blessing or gratitude in the experience.

After my daughter died, I thought I was broken and my life was ruined. How could this not be true? After all, everyone said losing a child was the worst thing in the world. I bought into that belief and for many years wore my badge proudly: mother of a dead child. When I was in a deep depression, I didn't know I had another choice. I became the woman I thought I had to be, depressed and damaged.

While sitting in a depression-support group, I realized I no longer wanted to be part of this "club." Some individuals had been participating in this group long before I joined. I didn't want to end up like them. I saw a window out of my depression and I leaped into a world of joy. For the first time in my life, I gave myself permission to feel joy.

I was now able to see the experience with Shannon from a higher perspective. I understood the lessons, the blessings, and ultimately the gift in the experience. No matter how awful we may judge our lives to be at any moment in time, we have all had moments when we've experienced love, connection, happiness, and joy. Sometimes we just forget.

This exercise is a reminder of those times. It's a way back into our loving hearts and a reminder that this is our true nature. All the other stuff is just our story.

Example: I am grateful for the life I have been given. The events I have found challenging have taught me a level of compassion and loving I never could have achieved otherwise.

Example: I am grateful for the love and intimacy that my spouse and I give and receive from each other.

Example: I am grateful for the joy and love that fill my life.

Example: I am grateful for the lessons I learned from the experience with my daughter Shannon.

Make a list of at least ten things you are grateful for right now.

Magical Moments

Some call it synchronicity. These are the times when events, desires, and opportunities seem to align themselves for our benefit. We are in the "flow" and life seems easy. We have all had these times and feelings, whether we have been aware of them or not.

As human beings, we are all connected, but our unresolved issues often get in the way and keep us from experiencing our oneness. When we can take off our masks, let down our walls, and open our hearts, magical moments are realized.

Feeling unsafe as I grew up, I learned how to put up walls around myself. I chose carefully who I would allow in, and then only so far. I didn't know I was keeping myself from experiencing a deeper connection of love and joy. I didn't know a deeper connection existed. This was how I lived most of my life.

When I consciously began to take down the walls, I opened up to a whole new way of living. It was as if I was seeing the world for the first time. I experienced higher levels of joy and deeper levels of love. My willingness to let go of what no longer served me allowed my life to flow with grace and ease.

As I continue to deepen my connection with others, nature, and the universe, magical moments become a regular part of my life.

Make a list of your magical moments. Come back to this list often, review it, and add to it. Create *new* magical moments.

Example: I was feeling sad and my white kitty, Kiki, jumped up on my lap and stroked my face with her paw. The love I received was magical.

Example: I hugged my friend's father, and in that moment I felt the familiar love I had for my father.

Example: Just as I was thinking I needed to call my sister, she called me.

Healing Actions

Self-Discovery Journal

Continue writing in your self-discovery journal. Remember to become present with yourself. Don't filter or censor your thoughts or feelings. Just let them flow directly from your heart, through your hand, and onto the page.

Meditation

Go to your sacred space or find a place in nature where you will not be disturbed. Light a candle and fill the space with gentle music. Center yourself in your loving heart. Close your eyes and take a deep breath from the bottom of your soul. As you breathe out, release any tension, upsets, or discomfort from your day. Breathe in loving connection to your spiritual source. Breathe out any negative thoughts or feelings. Do this several times. Sit quietly for a few minutes just noticing your breathing. Say to yourself, "I surround, fill, and protect myself with love and white light."

Think of one person, living or deceased, that you love. Place your hands over your heart and picture them peaceful, looking at you. Allow yourself to feel their presence, maybe even noticing their scent. Remember the moments you shared with this person that you are grateful for.

There is a reason they have joined you. They have a message of gratitude for you. Listen as they share from their heart this special message.

If there is anything you would like to share, do so.

When you feel complete, lovingly express your gratitude to the individual you invited and to your spiritual source for joining you to assist with this process.

Then wiggle your toes, shake your hands, and open your eyes. Allow yourself a few minutes to reflect on the process.

Inner Reflections

What would your life be like if you were able to let go of past judgments? Judgments about others? Judgments that you have held against yourself?

What will it take for you to integrate the self-forgiveness process into your daily life?

Is gratitude a part of your daily routine? What would your life be like if you lived from a place of gratitude? How can you create more of this attitude?

Are you open to experiencing magical moments?

Choosing to Be Free and Loving

And the day came when the risk to remain tight in a bud was
more painful than the risk it took to blossom.

—Anais Nin

Letting Go and Moving On

It's hard to move forward when you are holding onto the past.
In this chapter you will learn how to release your attachment
to the past once and for all. You will be better prepared to move
forward into a life of meaning and purpose, a life of your own
choosing.

It is not the events of our pasts that are the problem; it is our
thoughts and judgments about those events that hold us back.

Events are actually neutral. How we hold them inside gives them meaning. The thought about the event comes first, then the feeling. We assign a value to the experience, good or bad, pleasant or unpleasant, and then we experience the corresponding feeling. This process happens so quickly, we are usually unaware of the progression.

In the previous chapters we have worked extensively at untangling our thoughts and feelings. We have also worked to identify the patterns we have assumed in our responses to life events. In order to truly move forward, we have to complete any unfinished business we have with the people and events of the past. This includes the judgments we hold against ourselves. In the past, regardless of how you may have responded to certain events, you were doing the best you knew how, at that time, to keep yourself safe. You now have improved tools for processing life events that are in alignment with where you are today, emotionally, physically, and spiritually.

You have the opportunity to shift your consciousness to a more positive and uplifting way of being. Everything that has happened in your life has a purpose. You can learn something from every experience. You have learned what you like and don't like in your life, and how your actions produced the results you got. Sometimes we seem to have the same experience over and over, until we learn our lesson and go in a different direction. There is nothing wrong with this: the universe is a wonderful place. Our lives tend to stay in the same place until we are ready to learn a needed lesson, take positive action, and move forward.

Tool 11: Completion Worksheet

In this exercise you will be looking back over your relationship review chart. On the following completion worksheets, write a short description for each event below the loving line from your relationship review chart. Using all of the worksheets and lists you have already created (feelings map, reframing worksheet, woulda, shoulda, coulda, affirmation worksheet, self-forgiveness statements, gratitude, and magical moments), prepare your completion worksheet. While doing this exercise, you may become aware of additional feelings or statements. Include whatever is present for you while you are completing this worksheet. Repeat with each event from your relationship review.

EVENT:_____

Write a short **description** of the event:

Make a list of the **feelings** you associate with this event:

Write your **self-forgiveness** for this event (use a separate piece of paper as necessary):

Reframe the event in a way that shows how it was an opportunity for you to grow, learn or heal.

Find the **blessing and gratitude** for this event in your life.

Tool 12: A Completion Letter

In order to bring all of the work you have done to completion, this next exercise gives you the opportunity to bring closure to the unfinished business you have had with the person in your relationship review. You will write a letter to that person.

Set aside a minimum of one hour without interruptions to complete this. Focus on the emotional quality of what you write, not quantity. You might want to review your completion worksheets before you begin, so you can include those events that significantly affected your life. Make sure you use feeling words. It's about how you felt, not what the other person said or did that's important to communicate. Include the following elements in your letter:

Date

Dear (whatever name or label you call this person, i.e. Mom, mommy, mother, etc),

Begin with this statement: I was remembering some of the events of my life and wanted to share with you my feelings about them.

Include a minimum of three self-forgiveness statements.

Example: Mom, I forgive myself for judging you as …

Include what you learned about yourself or how you have healed as a result of the experience. Include a minimum of three.

Example: Mom, I wanted you to know …

Include a minimum of three blessings and gratitude statements.

Example: Mom, I am grateful for …

Good-bye, (their name).

I love you and miss you, but in order for me to be free I am releasing this energy and the negative judgments I have been holding onto. I release you and this energy up into spirit to be transmuted and returned as pure loving energy [or something similar].

(Your name)

Positive Rituals

You have done a tremendous amount of work releasing your past judgments, limiting your beliefs and stories. You no doubt feel much lighter. There is now space inside your life for new energy to come in. This space will fill. You can fill it with positive loving energy, or allow it to be filled by others or past negative behaviors. The choice is yours. This is your opportunity to create new positive and self-loving rituals. It may be hard to break old habits, but it is much easier to replace an old one with a new one. Fill this new and expanded space within you with loving by creating rituals that are self-nurturing and self-loving. Here are some commitments we recommend you focus on. Remember, what you focus on expands. Expand in loving.

Commitment to Self

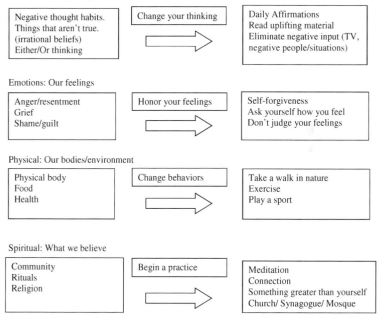

Mental: The way/things we think

| Negative thought habits. Things that aren't true. (irrational beliefs) Either/Or thinking | Change your thinking | Daily Affirmations Read uplifting material Eliminate negative input (TV, negative people/situations) |

Emotions: Our feelings

| Anger/resentment Grief Shame/guilt | Honor your feelings | Self-forgiveness Ask yourself how you feel Don't judge your feelings |

Physical: Our bodies/environment

| Physical body Food Health | Change behaviors | Take a walk in nature Exercise Play a sport |

Spiritual: What we believe

| Community Rituals Religion | Begin a practice | Meditation Connection Something greater than yourself Church/ Synagogue/ Mosque |

Healing Actions

Inner Reflections

Looking back over the work you have been doing, what has been your greatest shift? What has been your greatest challenge? How has your life changed? What is left to do?

What are some new and self-loving rituals you can commit to?

Conclusion

My (New) Life Is Just Beginning

> For yesterday is but a dream
> And tomorrow is only a vision;
> And today well-lived makes
> Yesterday a dream of happiness
> And every tomorrow a vision of hope.
> Look well therefore to this day;
> Such is the salutation to the ever-new dawn!
> —Kalidasa, Sanskrit poet and dramatist

In Conclusion

Over the course of this book, you have become aware of how the events in your life continue to influence the present. You have explored and become aware of feelings, beliefs, and memories. You have begun the process of owning both the pleasant and not so pleasant aspects of your past. You have accessed buried feelings, and explored and released judgments and negative feelings that no longer served you. Some of these feelings might have included shame, guilt, blame, or anger.

You have acquired tools that you can continue to use today and tomorrow: intentions, affirmations, compassionate self-forgiveness, reframing, free-form writing, meditation, journaling, and awareness of gratitude and magical moments.

You may be asking yourself, "How do I know when an issue is completely healed?" If you find yourself triggered by any aspect of an issue, that is a signal that healing work still needs to be done. When you are no longer triggered in any way by this issue and you can identify the lesson you have learned, then the issue is no longer an issue.

Be gentle with yourself. Emotions around holidays and anniversaries may still surface. Let that be okay. Don't judge yourself or your feelings.

Take a moment to acknowledge all the work you have done, the courage and determination that you applied to this process. Remember, the amount of healing you received has been, and will continue to be, equal to the level of your commitment and your willingness to go deep into your feelings.

Next Steps

You've awakened your soul on a journey, experiencing a new way of living. We encourage you to practice the tools you learned and integrate them into your daily life. We recommend that you continue to work with the person who came up for you the most in your work so far, before moving on to the next person.

Every time you repeat the exercises, you shift your energy to a higher level. When you no longer feel any upset or trigger regarding a person, move on to the next person in your life with whom you would like to bring closure. The more open and honest you are, the quicker you will move forward.

In our experience, we have found that doing this type of work in a group setting can have a greater impact on an individual's progress. The collective energy serves as a container for supporting and assisting the individual's spiritual self in moving toward a higher vibration.

It's important to remember to do this work at the heart level. It's easy to read books. That is a mental exercise and you will learn the philosophy of healing. You will talk the talk but not walk the walk. Deep inner healing takes courage and occurs when you work from your heart.

Make a commitment to letting go and moving on. There is more love and happiness in the world than you could ever imagine!

May your journey continue to unfold with grace and ease as you take your next steps forward.

10

Our Journey

B ill and Irene were happily married with two kids, a cat, a dog, and a lovely home in the suburbs of Los Angeles. They worked together at the local university where they had met and enjoyed spending family time together hiking and camping. Everything in their lives seemed to be going well, but that changed dramatically when their daughter Shannon was diagnosed with bone cancer. She was only eleven years old. Bill and Irene were swept up into the tornado of life, and when it was all over, they discovered a new way of being in the world.

Bill's Journey

To say that I didn't like the way I felt is an understatement. My wife had recently announced, "I no longer want to be married to you." So I moved out of the house to sleep on an air mattress in my brother's den. I saw no way out and no hope for the future. I didn't want to be alive. That wasn't the first time I'd had that thought.

When I was nine years old I found my father dead in his car. He'd had a massive heart attack. Scared and confused, I became quiet and ran away to hide. Being quiet and hiding became a pattern in my life. I was scared and confused for many years after my father died. I didn't see a bright, positive future for myself; I had no hopes or dreams. If that was all that my life was going to be, I didn't want to be alive.

No one taught me how to handle this kind of loss. Looking back, it seems the adults in my life at that time were more afraid of me than I was of them. They were unable to offer help. A well-meaning uncle pulled me aside and said, "You're the man of the house now. You have to take care of your mother." He is also the one who told me, "Your dad didn't suffer. It was as if he had just gone to sleep." For a long time after that I had a great deal of trouble sleeping. When I did finally get to sleep, I had nightmares. I didn't realize until many years later that I'd made some sort of link between sleeping and death. No wonder I had trouble sleeping.

Eventually I met a woman whose particular set of issues seemed to match mine. I was commitment phobic, and she was recently divorced with two young children. After we had dated for some time, she introduced me to her daughter Shannon, who was five. She was a beautiful child full of life and wonder. Her life was just beginning, and she saw it as a marvelous adventure full of promise and love. She was all of the things I had been afraid to be when I was a child. She captured my heart immediately.

Eventually Irene and I married, and together with Shannon and her younger brother Thomas, the four of us started our life together. About a year and a half after we were married, Shannon was diagnosed with cancer, and that began a new chapter in our lives. After a three-year battle with her cancer, she died on September 11, 1994. Again I began the process of grieving over the loss of someone I loved.

Irene and I went to a lot of support groups and sought help from other professionals, but most of it wasn't very helpful. We even went to some groups that believed that the loss of a child meant your life was over and that you could never be happy again. Well-intended professionals spoke with a subtext that the loss of a child meant we would never be whole, complete, or fully happy again.

We got on with our lives the way I suspect most people do: one foot in front of the other. Not seeing any real future for ourselves, we just tried to get through each day. We put on happy faces and did the best we could. September 11, the anniversary of her death, was a painful reminder of our loss, and so were Thanksgiving, Christmas, birthdays, and every other holiday. In fact, the last four months of every year became more and more difficult to face. There was always someone missing from the dining table.

Eventually, after about six years, my wife had a breakdown. She could no longer work and had terrible migraines on a daily basis. She lay in bed most of the day with a bandanna wrapped around her eyes. Again I was thrust into the role of caretaker, a role I knew all too well.

I continued going to work, keeping the household together, and caring for Irene the best I could, but I too began to wear down. I became more and more angry and resentful of having to take care of her, though I was not aware of those feelings at the time.

September was rolling around again, and we decided to go to the mountains to get away and do some fishing—anything not to be home on *that* day.

On September 11, 2001, we went to town to pick up some supplies. When we got to the store we saw how upset all the other people were. "What's going on?" we asked.

"Haven't you heard? There's been a massive attack on the World Trade Center in New York."

Of all of the days for this to happen, it had to be this day. I believe that was the final nail in the coffin of our marriage. Irene announced that we could no longer be married shortly after that.

Blindsided once again, I was lost and alone. At the time I thought the world would be a better place without me in it. The life I was living was too painful to continue. Our friends began choosing sides. Some of them offered some not-so-helpful words of encouragement and advice: "She's crazy." "You're better off without her." "That f—— b——, after all you did for her." "That's how all b——s repay your loyalty."

I had some colorful friends. Over time I learned that their comments told me more about them than helped me with my situation. Some were confused that I didn't want to hear them trash talk Irene. Besides not being helpful, I knew what life was like for her. I'd walked that path with her. I can't even image what it must be like for a mother to lose her daughter. I also intuitively knew that whatever pain and suffering she was going through had nothing to do with me. If I was going to survive and get on with my life, it was essential that I let all of that go.

What seemed like the end of my life was really only the beginning. I enrolled in a seminar with the intention of combating the terrible loneliness I felt. What I discovered was far beyond anything I had ever imagined. I found a new way of thinking about myself and my place in the world.

This started my inward journey toward discovering what really works in the world and how I could heal all of the scars and heartaches of my life. What I believed was the worst thing that could have happened to me—the separation from my wife—turned out to be the best thing that could have happened. It was the kick in the butt I needed to get moving and discover a life full of joy and loving. This was a life I had never imagined in my wildest dreams.

I enrolled in the University of Santa Monica's spiritual psychology program and continue with it to this day—to learn, grow, and heal all of the parts inside of me that are not in alignment with a loving life.

I learned a new purpose and meaning for my life. I learned to live a life of joy and loving. I learned that the universe isn't some cold, dark, and scary place that is against me. Everything, every event and experience, is an opportunity to learn and grow. I now share this with others, through speaking, workshops, and coaching tools and philosophy. I've learned to heal myself and live an abundant loving life.

Irene's Journey

I looked all around me. The house was almost empty. The movers had worked swiftly. I walked into the kitchen and placed the note I had written on the yellow-tiled countertop, writing his name on the outside. Feelings of sadness stirred inside me as I gently closed the door. After nine years, my marriage was over.

I was twenty-one when I got married the first time. It was a way out of a dysfunctional household. I didn't have the tools necessary to communicate effectively when I was married, but I know without a doubt that I did the best I knew how at that time.

Eighteen years later, I was facing the final hours of my daughter's life. It was early afternoon, and as I looked out the window, I was mesmerized by the gentle wind blowing through the trees. It had been three long years of medical visits, doctors, and surgeries, and now it was all coming to an end. It was as if Mother Nature was waiting and comforting me during this time. There was nothing I had to do, just be. What had become the focus of my life, my purpose over the past three years, was ending. The sun peaked out through the clouds, and my awareness returned to the room.

As Shannon lay sleeping in her bed, covered by her soft pink comforter, I looked around her room. Everything in the room projected back to me what was inevitable. The pastel balloons from her birthday party were drooping. The party had been a week ago, and the sounds of laughter were gone, replaced by the whirring sounds of the oxygen machine in the background. The bouquet of pink roses was fading, and some of the petals had fallen onto the beige carpet.

Books, dolls, and stuffed animals were everywhere. Strawberry Shortcake, Rainbow Brite, Care Bears, and Barbie dolls were still and quiet.

I was tired. My body ached and my eyes hurt from lack of sleep. The blue La-Z-Boy recliner I was sitting on was also my bed. I lifted up the wooden lever on the side of the chair to elevate the foot rest, and pushed the seat forward with my back and rear end to recline. I felt the temperature drop and reached for the light-green afghan my mother-in-law had crocheted. My body began to warm up as I melted into the chair, cozy and warm. Shannon's room became our room. There was no time for me or anyone else. All my focus had been on taking care of Shannon, and now all of that was about to change.

Our nine-year-old cat Sparky was stretched out on the bed next to Shannon, purring loudly. The two of them were always comforting each other and loving each other unconditionally.

Hanging on the white walls of her room were the brightly colored pictures she had drawn, some with captions. Drawing was her way of expressing her feelings for people she cared about. She didn't want us to worry or be sad. Through her pictures she encouraged us and let us know she was okay.

I held her hand as she slept and felt her dainty fingers begin to lose their warmth. It was just a matter of time now. I didn't want to let go of her hand. I didn't want to stop touching her for fear it would be the last time.

I was engulfed by a variety of feelings. Anticipation of what was going to happen. How would it end? Would it be dramatic, or would she go peacefully in her sleep? How would I react? Would I freak out or be able to deal with it? All of these questions were going through my mind. I had no control. I had to trust that everything would be okay.

I heard the sound of the microwave in the kitchen, and from the family room the noise of the television. Someone else was home now. Life continued outside Shannon's bedroom, and soon I would be joining in.

*   *   *

Two months after Shannon died, my mother died after battling Alzheimer's for five years. Two months after that, my father died of cirrhosis of the liver. Six years later I finally hit rock bottom and was diagnosed with major depression.

After six months of doctors' visits, therapy, and group work, I saw a window out of depression. I decided to live again. For the first time in a long while, I could actually feel my feelings. I wanted to live life fully. I didn't want to think about the past and I found myself increasingly angry at my husband. I blamed him for reminding me of the past.

I asked him for a separation and got involved with another man I had known earlier. I thought I could turn back the clock and become the person I was before all this bad stuff happened. Most of my friends thought I was crazy. I took a risk because I believed I was doing what was best for me.

During our separation, my husband shared with me the type of inner work he was doing. I was intrigued and decided to do some of the same work on myself. Four months later, we were back together. Our marriage had not only survived, it was stronger than ever. The separation had been a blessing in disguise for both of us.

I realized that my daughter's death had been the trigger for me to look closely at all of my inner wounds.

Over the last twelve years, I have continued to do the inner work. I became certified as a grief recovery specialist, returned to school to receive a second master's degree in spiritual psychology, received a certification in spiritual cleansing, and have participated in a variety of workshops and seminars.

Today, as a transformational life coach and workshop facilitator, I share with my clients my personal experiences and the tools and techniques that worked for me, in the hopes of making their journeys a little bit lighter.

Stafford Life Coaching

For information on our private coaching packages and upcoming workshops, please contact us:

Stafford Life Coaching
P. O. Box 642
Monrovia, CA 91017

www.staffordlifecoaching.com
www.fromheartachetohappiness.com

You mail also reach us by e-mail at: info@staffordlifecoaching.com